Ethics in Finance

Kara Tan Bhala

Ethics in Finance

Case Studies from a Woman's Life on Wall Street

Second Edition

Kara Tan Bhala
Seven Pillars Institute for Global
Finance and Ethics
Kansas City, MO, USA

ISBN 978-3-031-34400-8   ISBN 978-3-031-34401-5   (eBook)
https://doi.org/10.1007/978-3-031-34401-5

Cover illustration: Bespoke cover

This Palgrave Macmillan imprint is published by the registered company Springer Nature Switzerland AG
The registered company address is: Gewerbestrasse 11, 6330 Cham, Switzerland

PRAISE FOR *ETHICS IN FINANCE*

"Dr. Kara Tan Bhala has written a must-read for not only those considering a career on Wall Street, but also for any retail investor in this new era of social media led investing. The book is an honest and compelling read directly from Kara's experiences as a sell side analyst and a successful portfolio manager. The book offers riveting case studies from personal challenges that confront a woman striving to achieve in finance. The book is transformational: it places readers in real situations with diverse ethical challenges on Wall Street, and compels them to role play decisions from the inner conscience. One will journey beyond what is conventionally right and wrong, and delve into numerous ethical dilemmas and moral grey areas that professionals encounter on Wall Street."

—Sid Velakacharla, *Former Partner and Portfolio Manager, Indus Capital Partners*

"Kara Tan Bhala, through decades as a practitioner and theorist, creates the perfect vehicle for readers to appreciate real-life applications of ethical theory to financial situations. Many may view this chasm as too vast to conquer. But Kara's special synthesis of insight and pragmatism bridges the divide. This book really is a must read for anyone currently or soon-to-be in the financial profession, and for those curious as to why financial ethics is not an oxymoron."

—Warren Yeh, *CFA, Former Managing Partner, Adapa Partners (Long/ Short Pan Asian Hedge Fund)*

About this Book

Ethics in Finance earned five major awards: winner of the Business Book Awards (UK) 2022, and the Goody Business Book Awards 2022; silver medal winner, Global Book Awards 2022; bronze medal winner, Axiom Business Book Awards 2022; and finalist, International Book Awards (US) 2022. The book comprises multiple finance and ethics case studies. The second edition adds video summaries to each chapter. The purpose of the book is twofold. First, the case studies teach readers how to evaluate and determine resolutions to ethical issues in finance. Second, the reader enjoys a journey with the author, a woman, through her years working in finance. The case studies focus on ethical issues in finance which the author encountered over nearly a 30-year career in the industry. There are 10 cases extracted from different sectors of finance. This broad range is a consequence of the author's experience from almost all sides of the business: the buy side, the sell side, equity research in Asia, equity sales, mutual funds, hedge funds, the finance academy, and consulting. Each case study has an engaging narrative describing the background, transactions, players, and ethical issues. The ethical issue is analyzed and resolved using appropriate theories of moral philosophy. Descriptions and analyses are rigorous yet comprehensible, approachable, and entertaining. Apart from ethics determinations, the material in the book describes and explains a variety of specific, and even complex, financial transactions. Each case explains the roles of various players involved. In this way, readers learn about the work involved in different finance positions, from investment bankers and equity traders, to portfolio managers and equity analysts. Readers also get an understanding of major financial transactions and activities such as IPOs, secondary offerings, equity trading, and equity valuations. The book will appeal to the general reader, finance practitioners, college and high school students, and lecturers who can use it to supplement courses in finance or business ethics.

ABOUT THE AUTHOR

Dr. Kara Tan Bhala is President and Founder of Seven Pillars Institute for Global Finance and Ethics (USA), the world's only independent think tank for research, education, and promotion of financial ethics. She was an Honorary Research Fellow at Queen Mary University of London, and is a Jury Member for the Ethics and Trust in Finance Global Prize (Switzerland), and US Ambassador for the Transparency Task Force (UK). She has nearly 30 years of global finance experience through working on Wall Street. She also has owned and managed a small farm in Kansas. Dr. Tan Bhala has five degrees across three disciplines: a Bachelors (City, University of London) and Masters in Business (Oxford University), Masters in Liberal Studies (New York University), and Masters and Ph.D. in Philosophy (University of Kansas). She has lived and worked in London, Oxford, Singapore, Hong Kong, New York, Washington D.C., and currently resides in Kansas City. She is a member of America's Council on Foreign Relations and England's Royal Society for Asian Affairs.

For Shera, so she knows what I did before she graced our lives with her beautiful presence, and what I was doing between making her breakfast and serving her dinner.

Acknowledgments

I wish to thank Eric Witmer, who read my book proposal and encouraged me with genuine enthusiasm to embark on this project. This second edition owes much to his discerning editing of the first edition.

CONTENTS

Preface to Second Edition

Perhaps now more than ever, the global financial system needs ethics. A mere 15 years after the 2008 Great Financial Crisis, the system confronts an(other) impending global banking crisis. As I write this Preface to the Second Edition of *Ethics in Finance*, UBS, urged on—no, forced— by the Swiss National Bank, regulator Finma, and the Ministry of Finance, has offered to buy Credit Suisse shares for CHF 0.76 per share, a nearly 60 percent discount to Credit Suisse's last closing share price. Along with the international financial community, I watch live the hastily arranged, emergency Sunday press conference about the UBS rescue of Credit Suisse where regulators, government, and a somber UBS chairman try to calm slow churning fears. A wrong move, and global financial markets accelerate into a death spiral. To me and no doubt many others, this drama seems like *déjà vu*.

During the entire discussion, presenters spoke the word "confidence" distinctly more often than either "capital adequacy", or "liquidity". They focused on, indeed, agonized about, the collapse in "confidence" that would lead to a panicked bank run on Credit Suisse. Capital adequacy ratios were fine. Liquidity to the tune of CHF 50 billion had been provided by the central bank. Central banks upped their swap lines. But confidence stood to be the problem.

But on what is "confidence" based? That question was neither asked nor answered in the press conference from Berne. Let's be clear: confidence does not quantify into a convenient number inserted into financial models. Confidence in an individual, a company, a system, is grounded on trust. Who can we trust but those we consider trustworthy? And there's the rub. Trustworthiness is a virtue, explained by brilliant Aristotle as far back as the fourth century BCE. Virtues fall squarely into the province of Ethics. Ergo, Ethics trumps Numbers.

And yet, as Chapter 10 of this book illustrates, business schools in large part avoid teaching financial ethics because for these schools, Numbers trump Ethics. Over and over again, reality suggests otherwise. It's time (honestly, it was a long time ago) to re-evaluate the pitifully low priority given to teaching financial ethics in business schools. What about financial institutions? Have they blurred appearance and reality? Often, they pay lip service to ethics and engage in endless virtue signaling. Instead, they should demonstrate and practice ethics at the very top of their organizational hierarchy and hold their senior-most officials accountable when they fail ethically. And what about the regulators? Surely, they need to introspect about the extent to which they have been captured by financial institutions. All players need only survey the voyage toward destruction of a once-venerable symbol of Swiss identity, Credit Suisse, to grasp the value of ethics.

Credit Suisse, founded on July 5, 1856, fell because of repeated ethical failings. The bank, motivated by greed and seriously breaching its supervisory authority, invested in Greensill Capital, which collapsed in 2021. The cost: $10 billion. Just three weeks after the Greensill demise, Archegos Capital Management defaulted, resulting in a $5.5 billion write-down for Credit Suisse. Later the same year, Credit Suisse was fined $475 million by U.S. and British authorities for its role in a bribery scandal in Mozambique involving loans to state-owned enterprises (SOEs). This level of ethical failure invariably leads to confidence loss. Thus, it did not take much to topple the 167-year-old bank.

The immediate cause of the downfall of Switzerland's second largest bank began with the first domino in the 2023 banking eruptions, Silicon Valley Bank (SVB) in the U.S. A midsized bank that concentrated far too much of its business on tech startups and the tech sector. Few suspected the fall of one midsized bank would have a disproportionate effect on confidence in financial markets. Apparently, since 2008, the public has lost more confidence in the financial system, and the Establishment than many (including me) had imagined.

This surprising loss of trust is not trivial. Confidence in the global financial system is brittle, and the consequences, as demonstrated, can be catastrophic. Restoring a robust confidence in a shaken financial system requires heavy ethics work.

I wrote this book to contribute to the effort (dare I say struggle?). I am pleased those held in high regard have appreciated the contribution. The book has won five awards since the publication of the first edition:

- Winner in the International Book category of the Business Book Awards 2022 (U.K.).
- Bronze Medal in the Business Ethics category of The Axiom Business Book Awards 2022 (U.S.).
- Finalist in the Nonfiction Narrative category of the International Book Awards 2022 (U.S.).
- Silver Medal in the Business Ethics category of the Global Book Awards 2022 (U.S.)
- Winner in the Business Education category of the Goody Business Book Awards 2022 (U.S.).

I hope readers find this book as useful and engaging as the judges of the book awards.

Kansas City, USA   Kara Tan Bhala
March 2023

Introduction

Psssst. You, young people who want to be, or will accidentally end up, in finance, this book is mainly for you. When you enter finance, you will likely love the job, work entirely too hard, and encounter cases like the ones in this book. Ethics-laden situations require ethics reasoning and tools. I wrote these cases not as a record of my career but also as a way to help you, the future, to build a more ethical and socially responsible financial industry. Many of you will work in international finance and across diverse financial fields. To that end, this book is international in scope and covers a broad segment of the financial services industry. The case studies span across regions from a plantation in Malaysia, a hot social scene in Thailand, Christmas parties in New York, to suburban offices and college towns in the U.S. heartland. The industries range over a swathe of financial services: securities brokers, large asset managers, hedge funds, small mutual fund companies, and the finance academy.

I also wished to provide financial ethics guidance to the general public, including finance practitioners, policymakers, and regulators and to assure them human beings are morally educable. I try to do this through what I hope are engaging stories. The case studies form a narrative chain that represents a woman's journey through her career, inspired by Homer's Odysseus and his twenty years of (far more enthralling) travel after the Trojan Wars. Each case study starts with a story. Following the narrative, I highlight the prominent ethics issue in the case. For example, in Chapter 6 the ethics issue is quite clear: should a person engage in insider trading? I give reasons why insider trading has ethical implications. The section, "Ethics Analysis," then goes into details on the ethics tools the reader can use to analyze the issue. So, for example, using standard ethics frameworks, such as utilitarianism, we derive reasons why insider trading is wrong. The ethics analysis is followed by suggestions on how to resolve the problem and the best action to take. In sum, every chapter is an ethics training guide using case studies.

When I inform people I run a not-for-profit think tank that does research, education, and promotion of financial ethics, invariably the first skeptical response is, "Isn't financial ethics an oxymoron?" After a weary answer of "No, it's not an oxymoron, it's a necessity for the long-term proper functioning of finance and society," the next question usually goes, "But you can't teach ethics, can you?" That's when I get slightly more aggressive and say, "Well, should I have allowed my daughter to grow up feral then?" Meaning, do you as a parent, not teach your children how to behave well and about what is right and wrong, which by the way, constitutes the broad definition of ethics? If you do teach your children morality, then yes, ethics can be taught. This argument then elicits the riposte, "Well, you cannot teach ethics to adults, especially those already in the financial services workplace." My rejoinder at this point is "Why the arbitrary cut-off at 18 for an inability to learn how to be ethical? Why not 32 or 54? We find no problem teaching adults a bunch of other non-quantitative, values-infused subjects like religion, all forms of aesthetics like poetry and art, and, of course, self-help, and yet our ability to learn how to be ethical stops at the age of 18?" That's roughly a summary of my first day at a seminar where I give a lecture on financial ethics. I write this book partly to demonstrate financial ethics can be taught.

What should you take out of this book? First, don't seek perfection in the practice of ethics. Ethics is not a science with absolute right answers. Indeed, scientism has contributed to the decline of ethics education. In an age of science, people expect scientific-like demonstrations of reliability to solve important problems. Yet, the methods of science and the methods of ethics are different. Science uses the empirical method that involves experimentation and observation. The researcher gets data to support or refute a theory. Even though ethics does not use the scientific method it is no less rigorous. The method of ethics is discursive which means to proceed by argument and reason. The discursive method can be generalized as follows:

1. Give reasons to support a proposition about an act being right or wrong.
2. Analyze arguments.
3. Justify principles.

In the end, there may be good reasons to support an argument, but it may be difficult to persuade some people to agree with the conclusion. Most arguments are unlikely to receive unanimous agreement, but it is particularly vexing when examples given to support "proof" in ethics is impossible are the ones involving supremely difficult moral issues such as abortion or euthanasia. In practice, ethical issues are far more quotidian and uncomplicated. Aristotle understood the decision on the choice of a right act depends on the situation. A person needs to use reason and analytical tools to come up with the best ethical choice in that situation. Just because we cannot be perfect in every decision involving an ethical issue does not mean we should give up trying to think about and then to do the right thing. We are called to try our best, but we are not expected to be right all the time. This book aims to be your guide in ethics reasoning so you arrive at the right action.

Hopefully, you will be assigned the book in your business school classes. Maybe you will read this volume in your mandatory business ethics class (probably the only one you will have in your entire business major or MBA program). My backup plan if this book is not assigned by a multitude of college professors is to sell the rights to Netflix. (Failure to achieve this outcome with the First Edition, does not mean I have stopped trying.) The streaming giant will then produce a binge-able ten-episode series, which will subsequently rocket me into the ranks of the one percent. I was figuring Michelle Yeoh would play me. In the award-winning NBC comedy, *The Good Place*, Chidi Anagonye is a main character who is a professor of philosophy. In each episode, he teaches his friends some ethics theory so they can become good. And they do! So, just as *The Good Place* popularizes ethics, this book (and its film version, maybe) will, with luck, popularize financial ethics.

CHAPTER 1

Plantation Adventure Case Study

The Story: A Reverie of Somerset Maugham[1]

The segment of the financial industry that analyzes, promotes, and sells securities is called the sell side. This specific part of the business generates and sells its products to the buy side of the industry. Investment banks and stockbroking firms comprise the sell side and therefore, investment bankers, stockbrokers, and those who engage in securities analysis for these institutions are sell side professionals.

My first job in finance was as a sell side equity analyst based in Singapore, researching stocks in the Malaysian and Singaporean stock markets. The firm that hired me, to my surprise, was a blue-chip British stockbroker. The salary delighted beyond expectations and the work even seemed quasi-intellectual. I was ecstatic. Guanyin, the Bodhisattva of Mercy and Compassion, had answered my prayers. (A global bank eventually acquired the company, not an uncommon event among most independent brokers after the Big Bang in the U.K.) As a rookie analyst, my boss gave me the responsibility of covering the plantation and conglomerate sectors of these markets. My job entailed in-depth fundamental

Supplementary Information The online version contains supplementary material available at https://doi.org/10.1007/978-3-031-34401-5_1.

equity research on listed companies in these sectors and consequently, objective stock recommendations to our clients.

The plantation sector is distinctive to Malaysia. The country's exports currently comprise about 8% of soft commodities, palm oil and rubber, but in the late 1980s, the percentage was closer to 18%. At that time, the plantation sector constituted an important one for the Malaysian stock market. Six large plantation companies made up a significant combined market capitalization. The historical importance of this sector emerges from the country's economic development.

The Malaysian plantation industry started with British and other European colonizers planting cash crops such as oil palms and rubber. Henry Ridley, the Director of the Singapore Botanic Gardens encouraged the large-scale planting of rubber trees (*Hevea brasiliensis*) in Malaysia in the late nineteenth century. He had the avant-garde vision rubber would become important in the world economy with the advent of the motor car requiring rubber tires. In addition to encouraging rubber planting, Ridley was also responsible for developing the first systems of tapping the bark of the rubber trees in a way that maximized latex yield and minimized the consumption of bark.[2] British-owned estates grew a vast majority of the rubber. In the 1960s a shift occurred within the plantation industry from rubber to oil palms.

The oil palm, *Elaeis guineensis*, is a palm native to the tropical coast areas of West Africa. The first Malaysian commercial planting of 80 hectares took place in 1917 under the supervision of Henri Fauconnier, a Frenchman who established extensive rubber estates in northern Selangor before the First World War. Fauconnier planted his oil palms on Tennamaram Estate north of Kuala Lumpur, the Malaysian capital. Oil extracted from the oil palm fruit is called palm oil. Oil from the kernel or seed of the oil palm is palm kernel oil. Palm oil turns out to be an extremely versatile vegetable oil used in a multiplicity of products from doughnuts to lipstick. In recent years, oil palm has come under critical scrutiny because its cultivation is associated with deforestation, climate change, and destruction of wildlife species such as the Orangutan. Additionally, the oil is said to be uncongenial for a person's health.

Malaysia in the 1990s was an emerging market and economy. Most Malaysian plantations are run in the style of large agribusinesses but a handful of plantations are run by owners descended from a line that began with the original colonial planter who started the business. In the first year of my sell side and financial life, a rather venerable plantation company decided to do a secondary share offering. My company was chosen as broker for the offering and I was tasked with writing a research note on our client's plantation business. I needed to evaluate the company and make a recommendation to investors. Those in finance and law will understand when I say a "Chinese Wall" separates sell side equity research, and trading and sales in the same investment bank. The research generated by analysts such as myself ought to be objective and free from any influence from sales and trading desks of the same company. Indeed, the latter are not to even speak to analysts about the offering company in the period prior to and during a share offer. While aware of this particular conflict of interest, I had a rather vague notion of another source of conflict, which is the one between the needs of the company being analyzed and doing what is best for the clients of the research analyst. The client wants honest, dependable research while the offering company would like the most favorable review. Unsurprisingly, the two goals sometimes conflict.

One interminably marketed pitch of sell side research is the unique benefits of analyst visits to the company to "kick the tires" and get straight talk from management. I was young, energized, and eager to do insightful work. I packed my bags, readied myself for a tour of the plantation and an overnight stay at the home of the company's CEO, call him Paul, at his invitation. The walk around the oil palm trees was long and the weather turned out, as usual, to be hot and humid, but I was exhilarated. I studied the trees at various stages of growth, observed the health of the crops and saw how expertly the staff worked. I was impressed by the operation.

I returned to Paul's home for drinks and dinner. He and his wife had invited another couple and the man worked in a senior management position for the plantation. Paul's house could have emerged from a Somerset Maugham story set in the tropics, during British colonial rule. Attendants in white coats served us cold drinks on the capacious verandah at twilight, overlooking the darkening trees. Crickets chirped, the evening breeze provided welcome coolness. After drinks, we moved to the formal dining room for a delicious, house chef-cooked meal, all served by the same white-coated attendants. There followed port and after-dinner liquors in the parlor. My hosts were gracious, kind, and flatteringly attentive. I retired to bed feeling as if I had done a good job gathering relevant information and starting an honest, friendly working relationship with Paul.

The next morning, the same attendant dressed in his starched spotless uniform, served my hosts and me a fine English breakfast. What a glorious time for a young, impressionable equity analyst! I returned to the office rather chuffed that I could actually captivate the attention of such distinguished and influential people.

As I began writing and analyzing the company over the next few days, Paul called me to find out how the research was going. How was I? Did I enjoy the time at the plantation? Did I like the company? Were the financials excellent? What would my recommendation be? I felt uncomfortable with these queries because I vaguely knew my final recommendation for the stock had to be independent of my relationship with Paul. The romance of that Somerset Maugham evening could not cloud my decision. Despite the efficiency and well-managed nature of the business operation, I thought the stock was overvalued. I discussed this recommendation with my boss. I told him about feeling conflicted, as Paul had been so kind. Would I be betraying Paul if I gave the recommendation of "overvalued"?

ETHICS ISSUE: HONESTY IN EQUITY RESEARCH

Conflict of Interest

That question should, of course, be irrelevant to an equity research analyst when determining the recommendation on a stock. Indeed, my relationship with the staff and management of a company I researched should not influence any stock recommendation decisions. Otherwise, my objectivity as an equity analyst would be compromised. The ethical issue associated with this compromised position is called a conflict of interest. It just takes a second of reflection to realize conflict of interest is prevalent throughout business and politics because these are spheres of human activity that usually involve large sums of money. For example, at the highest level of state, should the former President of the United States have owned and operated a five-star hotel in Washington DC? As he was the owner of Trump International Hotel DC, foreign parties who wished to curry favor with the then President may have felt it was necessary to stay at the hotel. Residing at the hotel and paying high rates may have influenced Presidential decisions in favor of those who stayed or used hotel services. Even if the former occupant of the White House was not affected by emoluments from his hotel, there was always the temptation he would have been influenced sometime in his presidency. In addition, the existence of this conflict of interest taints that high office with corruption and corruptibility. As a consequence, people lose trust in their President. That is a bad outcome, from a utilitarian perspective.

At a more mundane but no less money-engorged level, investment banks prior to the 2008 Great Financial Crisis (GFC) operated with conflicts of interest on a regular basis and most likely still do so now. Goldman Sachs and the Abacus CDOs (Collateralized Debt Obligations) case comes to mind. On that deal, Goldman acted as agent for the buyer, Paulson and Co. and the seller, IKB, of a CDO. Was it arrogance, greed, or an ethically relaxed organizational culture that led Goldman to believe it could be an honest broker when acting for two clients on the opposite side of the same deal? There also was a conflict of interest because not only was Goldman acting as agent to Paulson and Co. and IKB, but it also was acting as a principal on its own behalf. When it comes to conflict of interest, one party serves two or more principals. Conflicts arise because the interests of the two principals likely are different. The pertinent question in a conflict of interest case is, how many masters can a financial institution honestly serve at one time? It is a wise biblical observation that no one can serve two masters (Matthew 6:24). When serving two masters at the same time on the same deal, a financial institution is unlikely to act honestly and transparently for both parties, treating each party equally. First, the financial gain from one of the parties is always more than the other. The sums of money involved are inordinately large. Second, the financial institution usually prizes one client relationship more than another because of past returns and expected future returns from that client. Big income generating and regular clients are favored over smaller, sporadic paying clients.

Ethics Analysis: Honesty and Integrity Are Virtues

Similarly, equity analysts cannot serve two masters—the management of the company they investigate and clients who rely on their good faith stock recommendations. The answer to the question I asked myself about whether it would be betraying Paul to give the stock an "overvalued" recommendation would be therefore, "No." I didn't have a moral obligation to Paul to do that which would please him. He treated me with warm hospitality, bringing me into his family circle, and as a *person*, I should be grateful for this kindness. However, as an *equity analyst*, I was not obligated to him. He provided me with the information about his company, in a pleasant way, no doubt, and it was my job to use this information, analyze the data, and come up with a rational recommendation based on a thorough and honest financial evaluation. My obligation as an analyst was to the clients who trusted in the objectivity of my research. As investors, they relied on the integrity of my research.

Aristotle

The virtue of integrity is tied closely with other virtues such as honesty and trustworthiness. As these virtues are relevant in this case study, we examine the ethics of the case through the lens of virtues and character. The Greek philosopher, Aristotle (384–322 BCE), stands out as one of the first thinkers in history to articulate a virtue ethics approach by devising and writing down a systematized theory of virtue ethics in his *Nicomachean Ethics*.[3] Aristotle rates as a genius, and it would not be an exaggeration to say he developed the very structure of philosophy as we now know and use. He was a student of the illustrious Plato, who was a disciple of the enigmatic Socrates, who chose to kill himself (by swallowing the poison hemlock) rather than be dishonest about his values.[4] Aristotle himself was a teacher, first teaching at the Academy, a philosophical school founded by Plato. At one point in his life, Aristotle was even tutor to the young heir of the Macedonian throne, the future Alexander the Great, a famous king who extended the Macedonian Empire across what is now Turkey, Egypt, much of Western Asia, and on into India. If Aristotle hoped to inculcate the virtues in the young Alexander, he did not achieve much success in light of the brutality of some of Alexander's campaigning tactics. Yet, the mighty king was not completely heartless. As he traveled across the world doing battle and conquering foreign lands, he would also collect samples of local flora and fauna and send them back to his esteemed teacher for study, besides being a brilliant philosopher, Aristotle worked also as a biologist and naturalist, applying a logical method to derive knowledge from empirical data.

After teaching at the Academy, Aristotle founded his own philosophical school in a public exercise park called the Lyceum. The students there came to be known as "peripatetics" from their custom of walking up and down (in Greek, *peripatein*) as they discussed their philosophical researches. The 11 years spent studying and teaching at the Lyceum were highly productive and happy for Aristotle. It was the time of his most enduring achievements. Alas, political upheaval disrupted his life when the Athenians saw a chance to rid themselves of Macedonian rule when Alexander the Great died at the young age of 32. In a wave of anti-Macedonian feeling, the Athenian political establishment charged Aristotle with "impiety," the same catch-all offense which led to Socrates' execution by suicide two generations earlier. Aristotle is said to have remarked that he chose exile "lest the Athenians commit a second sin against philosophy." He died the next year at the age of 62, from drowning.

Virtue Ethics

Virtue or *arete* translates into excellence, which makes sense because virtues are excellences of character. Utilitarian and deontological theories of ethics, which we talk more about in later chapters, evaluate an action to ascertain its moral worth. Utilitarian theory measures the consequences of an agent's actions. Deontological theory focuses on the principles of action, their universality, and justification. In contrast, virtue ethics focuses on the agent, the person who performs the action, in light of the circumstances and all of her other actions. According to virtue ethics, moral evaluation centers on the person's character, on the traits of character underlying the action. We call these character traits virtues.

There are two types of virtues: intellectual virtues and moral virtues. Intellectual virtues comprise excellences of the mind, for example, the ability to understand, reason, and judge well. Our school teachers, our parents, and our mentors teach us intellectual virtues. Moral virtues are dispositions we develop through habituation. In other words, we become virtuous by practicing the virtues. Examples of moral virtues are honesty, courage, integrity, trustworthiness, justice, and generosity. For Aristotle, humans are by nature, neither virtuous nor not virtuous. Instead, we have the capacity for virtue and are able to acquire them through habit. So, Aristotle's argument in the ageless debate of whether humanity is naturally good or bad is we are neither but have the capacity to be either. To ensure our capacity to be good is fulfilled, it is therefore crucial we acquire virtues through right training. Just as we become harpists by playing the harp, so too, "we become just by doing just actions, temperate by doing temperate actions, brave by doing brave actions" (NE 1103b1–2). Conversely, just as we have the capacity to become virtuous through correct training, we also may acquire vices through poor instruction.

If humans are morally neutral by nature but possess the capacity to be good or bad, then virtue can be taught through a method Aristotle calls habituation, which means we continuously practice virtuous actions until they become a habit. We have to keep doing virtuous acts in order to get into the habit of being virtuous. Practice is a vital part of virtue. We do not become good by merely examining what is good. Becoming virtuous requires us to be active. Aristotle is interested in behavior modification through action. By doing virtuous deeds repeatedly, our emotions are shaped to take pleasure in virtuous actions. The pleasure we obtain from virtuous actions in turn determines the desire of future actions so they align with the good.

Finance is a distinctive practice, and as such, we expect its ethical practice to be especially associated with some distinctive virtues. Honesty for example, is most important in every financial transaction. You would want a financial professional to be virtuous and exhibit honesty in everything she undertakes. The truly honest financial professional does not even think of cheating or lying. According to virtue ethics, the hallmark of a virtue is that it's ingrained in one's character. After years of cultivation and practice, honesty would therefore, seem perfectly natural.

Let's return to my Plantation Adventure and apply what we have learnt about virtue ethics. What should I have done when confronted with the choice of pleasing Paul or giving an "overvalued" stock recommendation on his company? I would have reasoned my way to a decision as follows: If I want to become a virtuous person, I would act the same way as a virtuous person. In this case, the virtuous person would not be influenced by the manipulative behavior of another more powerful person. Instead, she would have the integrity and honesty to write the research as she truly thinks. I should therefore, act in the same way. If I do, following the theory that virtue is a developed habit, it is more likely I will act with integrity in another new situation. I instill the trait of integrity through developing this virtue as a habit.

RIGHT ACTION: WRITE IT AS YOU SEE IT

It has been my good fortune to work with people who possess admirable integrity and have helped me make ethical choices. My boss, who also was under pressure by his superiors to provide a strong buy recommendation for the plantation company, advised me to release the research report with my honest recommendation. He would not be moved by the needs of the sales desk and I should not be swayed by the incipient friendship with Paul. We released the report with an, "overvalued" recommendation.

Subsequently, the sales team managed to sell every share of the secondary offering even with my research recommendation. I spoke to clients and told them exactly what I thought. The stock was overvalued but the management of the company was superb. Over the longer term the company would continue to perform because it treated employees with dignity and its management had decades of experience in the plantation industry.

Paul did not contact me again. For future research, I spoke to people who reported directly to him. The lesson in this case study is when doing sell side equity research, hold on to your integrity and give your honest, full-faith opinion on a stock, independent of external pressures. Support and moral guidance from allies in high places are invaluable.

NOTES

1. Somerset Maugham, *Maugham's Malaysian Stories* (Asia: Heinemann Educational Books, 1989).
2. Henry S. Barlow, "The Malaysian Plantation Industry: A Brief History to the Mid 1980s." Arabis. http://www.arabis.org/index.php/articles/art icles/plantation-history/the-malaysian-plantation-industry-a-brief-history-to-the-mid-1980s. Accessed on February 17, 2020.
3. Aristotle, *Nicomachean Ethics*, trans. Terence Irwin (Hackett Publishing, Indianapolis, 1999).
4. What we know about Socrates is mostly from Plato, although we also have some information about him from the works of Xenophon and Aristophanes. According to Plato, Socrates was tried by the Athenian state and found guilty of irreverence to the gods of Athens and corrupting Athenian youths. We are told that Socrates usually went around the *agora* (marketplace) debating with anyone who would engage with him, young and old, male and female, rich or poor, slave or free human, on first order questions like, "what is piety?", "what is the Good?", and "what is justice?" Eventually, all this questioning led to the questioning of established authority. In 399 BCE Socrates was put on trial and judged by a jury 501 Athenian citizens. The jury subsequently found him guilty of irreverence, a failure to show piety towards the gods of Athens. Socrates was sentenced to death. While he had a chance to escape and live a life of illegal exile, Socrates chose death because he did not wish to inflict harm on the city breaking the law. Thirty days after his trial, Socrates took the cup of hemlock (cheerfully according to the *Apology*, Plato's dialogue on Socrates' last days) and drank.

CHAPTER 2

Bangkok Misadventure Case Study

THE STORY: A SORDID REQUEST—TO DO OR NOT TO DO?

After working for a couple of years in equity research in Singapore, I moved to both a different location and a new job function. New York is the pinnacle of international finance rivaled only by the City of London. Once again, I could not believe my good fortune, getting a transfer to the bustling city to work on its famous (and now infamous) Wall Street. My boss in Singapore supported my transfer to the equity sales desk in the New York office. My new job entailed selling and buying shares of Malaysian and Singaporean companies for largely U.S. institutional investors. I moved into a tiny 500-square foot studio apartment (a palace!) and enjoyed a daily walk to the trading room of my company on the 42nd floor of the Empire State Building. Life was sweet.

Then I was hit by the reality of work in sales. The good salesperson should like talking to, dining, playing golf, and generally engaging with people. Constantly. The people are almost always clients who can add or take away from your sales revenue and therefore, your bonus. The salesperson/client relationship tends to be unequal. Preferably, clients should

Supplementary Information The online version contains supplementary material available at https://doi.org/10.1007/978-3-031-34401-5_2.

K. Tan Bhala, *Ethics in Finance*,
https://doi.org/10.1007/978-3-031-34401-5_2

like you and at a minimum, respect your views. It always helps your cause if you have a good track record of selling or buying shares for clients that make them money. A salesperson should be extrovert, enjoy social interaction, take rejection in stride and be always naturally networking. My more senior colleagues on the sales desk taught me the golden rule of sales is "Keep the client happy."

Client requests were usually work related. Most commonly, clients required more research from analysts in my company or primary research on an industry. Buy side equity analysts would ask for reams of data on their areas of specialty (remember, the time was before AI and Google Search, gasp). No request was too weird. For instance, an analyst wanted to know the global demand for condoms going back over two decades. The data were used to forecast rubber use and ultimately the stock valuation of plantations. Clients commonly requested introductions to the management of companies being researched. Equity analysts and portfolio managers prize direct communication with relevant company executives. It was a way to get information from those involved with day to day management of the company. Multiple client requests came in daily and everyone needed to have the information or meeting set up by end of the day. As a back-up to senior salespeople, who brought in hundreds of millions of dollars of revenues a month, I made sure client requests were met. A few requests were not work related but social in nature. For instance, client requests to obtain tickets for Broadway shows, the U.S. Opens, Super Bowl, Met Opera, and the like were not unusual.

My ethical problem arose one day when a client, who generated sizeable commissions for the trading desk, called. He wanted to set up a dinner appointment. I said, sure, no problem, with whom? He hmmed and haaed a while. I waited with pen poised to note down his wishes, and then satisfy them, because I was taught this is what salespeople do. He continued he had heard Bangkok was known for exotic Thai women. Could I arrange one to have dinner with him? Like, one of our local female Thai research analysts, who also happens to look good, I asked innocently (because I was then) with an awkward chuckle. He laughed in response in an equally strained manner. No, like a classy escort from a respectable and discrete agency, he said. Ah.

In those days Bangkok had a reputation for being a city where one could indulge oneself in unseemly ways.[1] This client, let's call him Bob, was married, but he rather liked his drink and was said to enjoy partying hard. I stood on the trading floor on the phone with an important client who had just asked me to set him up with a high-end prostitute, trying to quickly think what to say. I wondered if I should be a middleman for such a transaction, which, I told myself grumpily, was not in my job description. Is it right to set up a woman for this type of purpose, just so my team could be rewarded with more commissions from him? Did I mention the client was married? I spoke to a couple of trusted friends about the problem and both agreed I should tell my boss I was uncomfortable with this task.

Ethics Issue: Friedman and Free Markets

The client asked me to do a task that made me uncomfortable. This task was: *Set up my client with a high-priced escort in Thailand (herein called the Act)*. Fulfilling the request was not illegal but was it unethical? When I put this question to undergraduate business majors or MBA students in my financial ethics class, usually around 20% of the class deem the Act unethical. That leaves 8 out of 10 business students who think it is not unethical to set up a married client with a high-end escort in a foreign country. In general, those who responded in this way were the male students. The reasons they gave to support their views are grouped into three categories: (1) the Friedman argument, (2) the free market argument, and (3) the employment argument.

The Friedman Argument: There's No Need for Ethics

The argument is based on the free market economic theory of Milton Friedman who won the 1976 Nobel Prize in Economics. Friedman posited economics as a positive science, a value neutral and objective discipline. Economics, and its stepchild, finance, deals solely with facts, and confines itself to drawing empirically testable propositions from them. Finance professionals should not endeavor to offer normative, i.e., values-based opinions. The separation of facts from moral values is sometimes called the "Separation Thesis." Friedman gave the thesis his intellectual benediction in the context of economics. This brand of economics is therefore, independent of any particular ethical position or normative judgments. The market fully and effectively occupies the space of ethics judgments. This ideology is rampant in business schools across the world but most particularly in the U.S. Only recently, with looming climate change catastrophe and political upheavals caused by wealth and income inequality, have more innovative and respectably ranked schools begun to offer classes on corporate social responsibility, and look beyond the purpose of maximizing shareholder value. For Friedman, a corporation's prime goal is profit maximization and to this end, the firm just has to operate within the law and not break the rules of the game. In all other instances, the corporation must remain value neutral.

In accordance with this line of thought Friedman says, "Positive economics is in principle independent of any particular ethical position or normative judgments."[2] Cementing this principle in place, finance has as its foundational orthodox model, Modern Finance Theory (MFT). This theory is based on what is often termed, neo-liberal economics. Essentially, MFT comprises three models[3]:

1. The Efficient Market Hypothesis
2. The Capital Asset Pricing Model
3. Options Pricing Theory

MFT makes five major assumptions:

1. Economic agents are always rational.
2. Rational agents are purely self-interested
3. Rational agents aim only to maximize utility.
4. Utility is distilled to economic utility, *i.e.*, profits.
5. Therefore, rational agents aim to maximize profits.

These assumptions are, well, assumptions, originally made to simplify a complex world to aid in developing predictive quantitative models. Naturally, the assumptions do not capture the richness and complexity of the real world. For example, numerous experiments show people are not motivated purely by economic profit but also by values such as fairness and trust.

The assumptions of profit maximization behavior and of an efficient market have replaced any need for ethical discourse to resolve moral questions in academic finance. Hence, the conventional wisdom has been that markets decide efficiently, and ethics is basically meaningless and unnecessary in finance.

The Free Market Argument

Some students reasoned it is ethical to set up the rendezvous for my client because the U.S. and Thailand operate as free markets. This argument is closely tied to the Friedmanite position which asserts the best economic environment for profit maximization is a free market. Neoliberal economics celebrates free markets because they are seen as the most efficient means for resource allocation and price determination, and ultimately for sustained economic growth. In a free market, government intervention is kept to a bare minimum. Price discovery and resource allocation are done through the forces of demand and supply. The high-end escort offers her services freely and the price she charges is driven by market forces. The client stands on the demand side of this equation and will accept the price if he is willing to pay. This transaction is one of millions in a free market and we do not need to intervene with ethical stop signs. Indeed, we are reducing a woman's earnings from her work.

The Career Suicide Argument

I suspect the two rationales above gave theoretical cover for the real reason many students said this case did not pose an ethics issue. They simply feared being fired for not complying with a client's request. Finance jobs in top investment banks are difficult to obtain and highly prized. Few would jeopardize their positions by taking a stand on a matter of ethics. Some students felt they would be close to powerless to do anything to oppose the client, being so low in the organizational hierarchy. The students played out the following doomsday scenario: the client would complain to senior management and threaten to withhold or reduce business to the investment bank. The concern about the potential loss of revenues would be enough to make management demand the student carry out the task. If she demurred, they would take note of her as a troublemaker, not give her choice clients in the future or keep her in mind for promotions. At best, her career in the firm would languish and at worst she would be fired.

In coming to this conclusion, the students were actually carrying out a quick utilitarian analysis and found the bad outcomes outweighed the good outcomes. Roughly, their mental calculations went something like this:

The Act: Set up my client with a high-priced escort in Thailand

Good outcomes:

1. I keep my job
2. I do not damage my career prospects at the company
3. I get more commissions from this client

Bad outcomes:

1. I may be allowing a woman in Thailand to be sexually and economically exploited
2. I am complicit in a husband cheating on his wife

Weighing the good and the bad outcomes, students concluded the good outweighed the bad and therefore, it is ethical to arrange the date for the client.

ETHICS ANALYSIS: FREE MARKETS, MARKET FAILURES, AND VALUES

Let's analyze the three arguments to check their moral reasonableness and standing. First, Friedman's argument that there is no need for ethics merits little weight as a justification of the Act as ethical. The assumptions about profit maximization and *homo economicus* being rational and self-interested are mere assumptions, not true statements of facts about the world. With the passage of time and constant use, these assumptions morphed from "let's assume," to "this is how it is," and then to, "this is how you ought to act."

Thus, assumptions underlying MFT have evolved from:

- "assume" (*assume* agents are rational, self-interested, and aim to maximize profits) to,
- "is" (agents *are* rational, self-interested, and <u>do</u> aim to maximize profits) to,
- "ought" (agents *ought to be* rational, self-interested, and *ought to* aim to maximize profits).

Ironically, *the assumptions have become the ethic*. Despite protestations of MFT proponents about the value neutral stance of finance theory, MFT comprises a set of values which in essence are: trust the efficiency of markets and maximize profits.

MFT has served us well in systemizing a broad field and providing a simple framework but the theory and its assumptions have become entrenched and attained a vaunted status as the truth in business. Since the 2008 Global Financial Crisis (GFC), questioning the primacy of neo-liberal economics-based finance theory has begun. Practitioners are more willing to speak of ethics in finance, urged on, no doubt by regulators and the public. In the meantime, because change in the academy is slow, business schools continue to teach these tenets of MFT as foundational belief concepts to young minds eager to be successful in business and finance. It's not a surprise when students say in my financial ethics class (subsequently canceled by disapproving, all male finance professors—more on this story in Chapter 9), it is not illegal to set up my married client with a high-end escort in Thailand, and one can do so without any qualms.

The second reason proffered by students for the act being ethical is we operate in free markets. There is a close relationship between this argument and the Friedman argument because free markets efficiently determine prices and resource allocation based on the forces of demand and supply.[4] The free market with its assumptions of profit-maximization as a goal and an all knowing, providential market has replaced any need for recourse to moral philosophy to resolve ethical questions in finance. There are remarkable parallels between the ideology of the free market and the God of the major monotheistic religions. The Mosaic God is omniscient (all knowing), providential (all good), and omnipotent (all powerful). Compare this characterization with the personality we ascribe to the free market: (1) "All information is already in the market" constitutes the principle of the efficient market hypothesis (all knowing); (2) The consequences of allowing the free market to work are the maximization of efficiency and profits (all good); (3) There is no way to outperform the market, either by active portfolio management or by government planning (all powerful). No wonder there is such idolatry of the free market!

Yet, we have witnessed market failures over the past few decades. In market failure, the individual incentives for rational behavior do not lead to rational outcomes for the group. In other words, the individual acts in her own self-interest but this act leads to poor outcomes for the group. An instance of market failure is negative externalities. As a result of burning fossil fuels over more than a century, there has been a build-up of carbon dioxide in the atmosphere. This increased level of CO_2 has led to increasing global temperatures. Climate change is thus a result of market failure.

Consider the number of financial crises from the 1980s to the present. Every bubble crash disproves the efficient market hypothesis (EMH). EMH is the cornerstone of MFT and the theory emerges from free market principles. Simply put, EMH states that stock prices already reflect all available information. The market has information on the economy, industries, and firms. Prices move as a result of this knowledge. There are numerous studies that disprove EMH which, are beyond the scope of this book. To argue against efficient markets, one needs to only consider financial crashes. During the housing bubble of the 2000s, it was not rational for house prices to triple in 10 years. Bubbles, as well as the crashes that follow them, do not reflect rational economic agency because they do not reflect correct prices representing all available information. Bubbles illustrate irrational expectations that arise when investors herd into the same investments at the same time. In these moments in history, greed, not rational expectations, drive prices. Over the past thirty years we have been victims of the following crashes:

- 1984 Savings and Loans Crisis
- 1989 Junk Bond Crisis
- 1992 Japanese Market Crash
- 1994 Mexico Currency Crisis
- 1995 Barings Securities Collapse
- 1997 Asian Currency Crisis
- 1998 Russian Currency Crisis
- 1998 Long-Term Capital Management Bailout
- 2007 Bear Stearns Collapse
- 2008 Global Financial Crisis
- 2020 Pandemic Crash
- 2023 Silicon Valley Bank Crisis

According to Paul Krugman, bubbles and crashes are proof of the fallibility of free markets.[5] If market failures do occur, then we cannot assume everyone who enters into a transaction does so freely or with the same level of economic power. We can therefore say quite reasonably the escort in Thailand may not be able to enter into the transaction with my client freely and with equal economic power. She may instead be a victim of economic exploitation.

The third reason my students give for fulfilling the client request is not based on any high minded financial or economic theory. They simply fear being fired from the job. If in the same position, many would do what is asked of them because they feel they have no choice. The students did a quick mental utilitarian calculation (see section "The Career Suicide Argument") and arrived at the decision to do the Act. The students were however, less than objective when they found that good outcomes outweighed the bad ones. Crucially, one of the key rules of utilitarianism is the decision maker must be completely impartial. Classical utilitarianism has these three principles:

1. Actions are to be judged right or wrong solely on the consequences of the actions.
2. To assess consequences, only the amount of happiness or unhappiness created is considered.
3. Each person's happiness counts the same.

The objective aspect of utilitarianism comes from the notion that each person counts equally, and everyone has an equal right to happiness, irrespective of her situation. Let's evaluate the utilitarian calculation again, this time with a higher degree of objectivity.

The Act: Set up my client with a high-priced escort in Thailand
Good outcomes:

1. I keep my job
2. I do not destroy my career prospects at the company
3. I may get more commissions from the client.

Bad outcomes:

1. I may be allowing a woman in Thailand to be sexually and economically exploited
2. I am complicit in a husband cheating on his wife.

In the utilitarian procedure above, at least two people may be harmed, one physically. In contrast, only one person enjoys the possible benefits. Weighing the amount of happiness versus the amount of pain, an impartial decision-maker would find the Act unethical. In addition, the calculation is too simplistic because the students simply presume they lose their jobs if they do not perform the task. Yet, the choice is not a binary one: do the deed and keep the job; or reject the deed and lose the job. A third choice may be added: discuss my reservations about doing the deed with a senior manager, preferably my direct boss. Tell her why I am concerned about the Act, giving all the reasons listed in the utilitarian evaluation. Indeed, discuss this ethical problem with friends, colleagues, and anyone else I trust. Get their opinions on what I should do. There may be someone who has gone through the same type of situation and can offer helpful advice. In these situations, it is best to not approach the problem alone and to understand others may share the same moral hesitation or have been in similar situations. Discussion and gathering opinions are useful processes for gaining mental and emotional support.

If I had financial ethics training at that time, I would have reasoned about the ethics of the Act as follows:

1. It is unethical to use a person as a means to your own ends (deontological moral principle).
2. I would be facilitating the use of a woman in Bangkok to fulfill the physical desires of a married man.
3. I was doing it to increase the chances of getting more business.
4. Therefore, I would be using a human being to achieve my own ends.
5. Therefore, according to (1) I would be doing something unethical.

Of course, I did not have the training or experience to reason in this way. All I knew was I had a nagging uneasy feeling about doing the action asked of me.

RIGHT ACTION: VALUES IN FINANCE

The head of the sales desk who happened also to be the executive manager of the New York office, was a hard-charging salesman. I went into his office to discuss my reservations about the Act with him. My nervousness was obvious from my voice which shook despite my attempts at evenness.

I must have looked like a young, anxious mess. It's so difficult to be ethical! My boss gave me a quizzical look after I had unburdened my conscience to him. His mental gears worked for a mere few seconds and then to my surprise he said he understood my misgivings and I did not need to do what was asked. I was relieved. Then in the next moment I worried about how to inform the client about this decision. I need not have been concerned. My boss gave the ignoble task to a senior salesman who fulfilled the request without a second thought. One lesson learned is, if your conscience bothers you about some act, pay attention. Speak to close friends or family and get trusted advice. You do not have to cope with ethical problems alone.

NOTES

1. As evidence of the continuing stereotype of Thai women's subservience witness the prostitution activities at the so called, Orchids of Asia Day Spa in Jupiter, Florida. This establishment was ostensibly a "Thai massage" place where Bob Kraft, the owner of the New England Patriots, was caught for solicitation and receiving sex acts. https://www.vanityfair.com/news/2019/03/patriots-owner-bob-kraft-truly-sorry-he-got-caught-in-prostitution-sting.
2. Milton Friedman, "The Methodology of Positive Economics." In *Essays in Positive Economics* (Chicago, IL: University of Chicago Press, 1966).
3. Kara Tan Bhala, "The Philosophical Foundations of Financial Ethics." In Costanza A. Russo, Rosa M. Lastra, and William Blair (Eds.), *Research Handbook on Law and Ethics in Banking and Finance* (Cheltenham, UK: Edward Elgar Publishing, 2019), 7–8.
4. Kara Tan Bhala, "The Consequences of MFT." Seven Pillars Institute for Global Finance and Ethics. https://sevenpillarsinstitute.org/mission/ . Accessed January 15, 2021.
5. Hersh Shefrin and Meir Statman, "Behavioral Finance in the Financial Crisis: Market Efficiency, Minsky, and Keynes." In Alan S. Blinder, Andrew W. Loh, and Robert M. Solow (Eds.), *Rethinking the Financial Crisis* (Russell Sage Foundation, 2013), 110.

CHAPTER 3

Hong Kong Hike Case Study

THE STORY: THE PRESSURE TO PERFORM

The so-called "buy side" of finance comprises investment management firms such as pension funds, hedge funds, mutual funds, and investment divisions of insurance companies. These institutions manage money for other people. I worked as a buy side equity analyst evaluating Asian stocks at a private bank in New York and then as a senior portfolio manager at a top five (by assets under management or AUM) fund management company (the Company).

I was fortunate the Company chose me from hundreds of candidates to start and manage its Far East ex-Japan mutual fund (the Fund). This portfolio designation sounds fancy, but it simply means the Fund was allowed to only invest in equities of Asian-based companies, except for those companies listed in Japan. Thus, the Fund invested mostly in equities trading in Taiwan, South Korea, Hong Kong, China, Indonesia, Philippines, Singapore, Malaysia, Thailand, Vietnam, India, Sri Lanka, Australia, and New Zealand. I stepped into this investment scene at a fortuitous time. The last decade of the twentieth century was a period in

---

Supplementary Information The online version contains supplementary material available at https://doi.org/10.1007/978-3-031-34401-5_3.

U.S. investment history when American investors became enamored with Asian equities. The Fund was one of the first of its kind: a mutual fund focused on investing in Asian ex-Japan equity markets. When the Fund first opened to new investors in 1992, US$250 million flowed in within one morning, which was a considerable amount at that time. The Company's management decided to close the fund at $250 million to allow the Fund's team to fully invest the money over time and after careful analyses, into the markets. Every time we opened the Fund up to investors, hundreds of millions of dollars would pour in within a few hours so that we had to close the Fund again. Subsequently, after a few iterations of this process, the fund grew to be the second largest Asia ex-Japan fund in the world with over US$1 billion under management.

The Fund also became one of the most high-profile ones in the Company's stable of mutual funds because of its presence in the emerging markets space, and also because Asian markets were supercharged at that time. In 1993 the Fund was up an unprecedented 87%, the best performing fund since, well, forever. In the same year, Hong Kong's Hang Seng Index was up 114%, the Philippines Stock Index was up 112%, and Singapore's Straits Times Stock Index was up (a mere) 46%. Global investors could not get enough exposure to these Asian "Tiger" markets. This sort of extraordinary market performance and greed inducing returns occur infrequently but not uncommonly in stock markets. Before the Asian Tigers stock markets boom, there was the Japanese asset price bubble or *babaru keiki* (bubble economy) in which real estate and stock market prices became highly inflated. In the short seven years from 1982 to 1989, Japan's Nikkei 225 Index went up a breathtaking 385 percent. After the Asian Tigers boom, the U.S. stock market had its dot-com bubble. In 1999, the peak of this bubble, the Dow Jones Industrial Index went up 25% (it subsequently went down for the next three years), a considerable move for a mature market. These stock market highs reflect periods of "irrational exuberance," a phrase coined by Alan Greenspan, a former Chair of the U.S. Federal Reserve Board, to mean highly overvalued asset markets, i.e., speculative bubbles.

During these bubbles, investors clamor for the asset that is rising at blistering speed and in seemingly unstoppable fashion. During the Asian stock market bubble, this level of exposure on the Fund, naturally, puts enormous pressure on the people managing the fund and especially on the portfolio manager who has ultimate responsibility. Daily public disclosure of performance, constant monitoring by financial consultants and their clients can loosen a portfolio manager's moral moorings. Speculative bubbles are, after all, driven by greed, a vice worthy of inclusion in the Seven Deadly Sins. A conversation with a famous football commentator and former NFL quarterback and a chat with an incensed former Governor of a Western state were among some memorable calls I had to field. Each wanted to know why the Fund had declined in performance and when returns would become positive.

At the end of one poorly performing year, I was tempted to "window dress" the portfolio. Mutual funds and portfolio managers use the strategy of window dressing to improve the appearance of a fund's performance at the end of the year or quarter. It is a technique to dress up the performance of a mutual fund at a particular instance but the longer term effects on a portfolio are typically negative. Portfolio managers resort to this practice when the fund's performance is lagging. In this case, window dressing involved putting buy orders without limits on purchase prices, for a number of thinly traded (illiquid) stocks already held in the Fund. These so-called "no limit orders" tend to push up prices of the illiquid stocks thus improving the performance of the same stocks held in the fund. The effect is enhanced if the portfolio holdings happen to be large. If these orders are placed on the last few days of the year, the rise in prices of the same holdings in the fund increases the fund's net asset value. Engaging in window dressing for year-end measurement purposes artificially pumps up fund performance. Other labels for this practice are, "portfolio pumping," "leaning for the tape," and "marking up." These terms refer to quarter-end and year-end price manipulation on the part of fund managers via the excessive buying of securities they already own. The idea is that excessive buying on the last day of the year inflates the fund's closing net asset value (NAV), which in turn exaggerates the fund's performance.[1] Research provides evidence of portfolio pumping, where both fund NAVs and the share prices of stocks widely held by funds are inflated on quarter-end, and especially on year-end, days.[2] Another recent study finds similar inflation in stocks widely held by hedge funds.[3]

Illiquid shares of small companies are prevalent in emerging markets such as Hong Kong. For example, let's say the Fund holds three stocks: Johnson Electric, ASM Pacific, and Giordano Holdings. Johnson Electric manufactures micro-motors such as the ones you find in a car's power steering or in electric fans. ASM Pacific manufactures tools, materials, and machines that make semiconductors. Giordano Holdings is a casual apparel retailer, selling mainly polo shirts, tee shirts, jeans, and shorts.

At that time each was a small cap stock, with low volumes of trading each day. A large order to buy these stocks could push their share prices up considerably. Say I put in orders to buy millions of dollars worth of each stock without price limits. I tell my trader to buy as aggressively as possible. These trades, when put through the market, are enough to boost the price of each stock by 10 to 20% in one day. If all three stocks go up this amount, then the effect on the NAV of the Fund would be significant on the upside. The more stocks are artificially traded up, the higher the NAV of the Fund at the end of the year. This is classic portfolio pumping.

The pressure to perform, the spotlight on the Fund, and perceived high expectations drove me to consider taking this step. As we shall reason in the next section, the act is unethical. It would be hard for a reader or student in the field to discern this assessment by only reading the academic finance literature on this topic. Instead, finance academics focus on the effects and methods used in manipulating prices (lots of statistical modeling involved for "scientific" legitimacy), but not on the ethics of engaging in these practices. In any case, under the pressure to perform, I asked my closest associate in the Fund, a senior research analyst, to put in the orders to buy illiquid shares of a handful of small Hong Kong companies we held in the portfolio. The no-price limit order would reap a significant price hike in those Hong Kong shares. My colleague looked at me anxiously and questioned if it was necessary to go down this road. I glared at him and getting no reply from me, he left my office.

Ethics Issue: Cheating Our Way Up

The primary ethical failing in this case is dishonesty. The dishonesty manifests as cheating. The cheating takes the form of manipulating stock prices to improve the year end fund performance. Indeed, portfolio pumping may even result in the fund outperforming its benchmark index. Relative outperformance is desirable because mutual fund managers are generally not assessed by absolute performance but by how well their funds perform against an agreed upon index. Through portfolio pumping the manager looks as if she's doing a fine job and then is able to profit from the outperformance through bonuses paid to her. The medium- to long-term performance of the fund did not require an increase in holdings of the illiquid stocks. The intention of the moral agent was not to improve the performance of the fund to benefit shareholders, but to falsely increase the fund's value in the short term to forestall criticism of performance, make her fund skills look good, and profit from that performance. Intention is an important factor when using deontological methods to assess the ethical value of an act and we discuss this point at greater length in the next section. Finally, take note that a portfolio manager who runs money for other people, whether through a mutual fund, hedge fund, or private brokerage account, has a fiduciary responsibility to the people who entrust their money with the manager.

ETHICS ANALYSIS: WHAT WOULD KANT SAY?

In this case, we use a deontological assessment to determine if, and reason why the act of window dressing through portfolio pumping is unethical. Deontology is philosophy's technical term for "duty based." *Deon* is the Greek word for duty and *logos* means science. The prime directive of deontology states we are morally obligated to act in accordance with a certain set of moral principles and rules regardless of the outcome. If the set of moral principles has a rule which says, "do not lie," then according to deontological ethics, we are obligated to not lie. There are no excuses, no exits, we must follow the moral rule and never lie. The fundamental foundation of the system is obviously, the set of principles. The crucial aspect of the said set of principles is how the principles come to be determined. The two major ways for attaining a set of moral principles are (1) through divine command and (2) through human reason.

Accordingly, there are broadly two systems of deontological thought. In religious deontology, so-called divine command theory, the moral principles derive their foundation and legitimacy from divine commandment so that under religious laws, we are morally obligated to either perform or not perform a particular act. It is worth noting the major religions, Christianity, Judaism, Islam, Buddhism, and Hinduism each have a set of moral principles which believers are called to follow. For instance, the Ten Commandments of the Old Testament command us not to, among other things, cheat, lie, covet (spouses, houses, slaves, or anything else), or commit adultery. Under Islamic moral principles, Muslims are called, for example, to be charitable to the poor, to not drink alcohol, and to not cheat. Buddhists have teachings they know as the Dharma that tells them to be generous, give to the poor, and to not cheat. You get the idea. The thing to understand is these principles are sourced from God or a divine entity. Clearly, deontological ethics has existed for millennia, since the dawn of human religions. Indeed, the first rule of ethical behavior many people around the world learn is from the religion in which they are raised.

There also is a secular, i.e., non-religious, version of deontology. Immanuel Kant (1724–1804) was the master designer of this version which we now commonly use in ethics evaluations. A brief history of philosophy necessarily goes through the works of the giants in the field. They are (arguably, because philosophers argue all the time): Plato and Aristotle (ancient philosophy), Thomas Aquinas (medieval philosophy), Immanuel Kant (modern philosophy), Friedrich Nietzsche (postmodern philosophy), and Ludwig Wittgenstein (analytic philosophy). Each, except (arguably) Wittgenstein, wrote extensively on ethics. Kant is, therefore, a towering figure in philosophy.

While Kant's work is monumental, his life was strikingly pedestrian. Kant was born in Konisberg, Germany, the fourth of nine children, of working-class Lutheran parents. He also died in Konisberg and in between his birth and death lived only in…Konisberg. He was first a tutor at the University of Konisberg, and then a professor of logic and metaphysics. In 1796 Kant gave up his lectures for reasons of old age. In 1798 his health began to decline and in 1804 he died in a state of senile dementia.

Kant was unusually small, thin, flat-chested and his right shoulder was higher than his left. Kant remained a bachelor, living alone with a manservant, and only at the age of 63 did he hire a cook. Before that he ate out, but rarely alone, invariably inviting guests to his midday meal. He was on the verge of marriage on two occasions but took so long to decide that the exasperated women left him for others. Kant was so attached to Konisberg by affection and habit that he could never make up his mind (not unlike Chidi Anagonye, also a professor of philosophy, of the NBC comedy, *The Good Place*) to accept any of the brilliant offers made him by other universities. In declining, he asked indulgence for his "temperament that cannot resolve to make changes which seem trifling to other men."[4] Kant never took a trip worthy of the name and ventured slightly beyond the borders of East Prussia once in his life. He owed his wide knowledge of the world to his constant reading and his imagination. When an Englishman visited, Kant spoke so vividly of St. Peter's that the gentleman was convinced Kant had been to Rome. Lest we imagine Kant to be dry and cold, we can take note that the likes of Herder and Hamann commented on the philosopher's good cheer and spirit, so much that he became one of the most popular citizens of Konisberg, welcomed everywhere for his grace, wit, and ready conversation.[5] Nor was he a boring lecturer. By all accounts, Kant was an excellent orator who excited his audience, even moving them to tears when he spoke about ethics.[6] I think of this Kantian achievement every time I give talks on financial ethics. As yet, as far as I know, not one person to whom I have lectured has been moved to tears.

Some may say Kant's system of ethics has a beauty and logic that really does move the soul. The key components of his duty-based ethics are the will, human rationality, the categorical imperative, and human freedom and dignity. Human beings develop a set of moral principles, i.e., rules, aided by human rationality. Instead of a divine being handing down the rules to us, we determine the moral principles using our own human reason. These principles must conform to a set of criteria Kant provides as measure and guide. It's genius, if abstruse. But here goes anyway. He calls the *measure* of a proposed moral rule, the categorical imperative. In high philosophical jargon, categorical implies a person is absolutely bound by her moral duty to abide by the moral rule. There are no excuses, no way to bow out of the duty. Imperative implies a command. Thus, the categorical imperative is an adamantium duty to abide by a command. It is a binding force for any person, irrespective of her interests or inclinations.[7] In drawing up a list of moral rules, we must measure each rule against the criteria contained within the categorical imperative. We can regard the categorical imperative as the ultimate principle against which all moral rules such as "do not kill" or "do not cheat" must conform to. If each rule checks out against every criterion of the categorical imperative, then it is an acceptable moral rule in a Kantian framework of ethics.

The first criterion of the categorical imperative is that a moral rule must be able to be made into a universal maxim to which all rational beings will agree. The second criterion is that a rule must respect the intrinsic worth or dignity of people. Kant believes people have dignity because they are rational agents, free and capable of making their own decisions, setting their own goals, and guiding their conduct by reason. The only way moral goodness can exist is for rational beings to act from a good will—that is, to know what they should do and act from a sense of duty. The third criterion is that a rule must treat people always as an end and never as a means only. To treat people as ends requires treating them with respect. Thus, we may not manipulate people, or use people to achieve our goals, no matter how good those goals may be. Treating people as ends, and respecting their rational capacities, means we cannot force adults to do things against their will, instead we should let them make their own decisions.

Using Kant's system, let's test the moral rule: "do not cheat," relevant in this case study, against the three criteria of the categorical imperative to see if the rule is legitimate. In the last section, we have already determined that manipulating prices through portfolio pumping is a form of cheating. First, can the rule "do not cheat" be made into a universal maxim that all rational people can agree upon? Yes, because all rational people would not want others to cheat on them. Second, does the rule respect the human dignity of others? Yes, because cheating on another would be denying respect to the dignity of that person who is cheated. Third, does the rule treat the other person as an end rather than a means? Yes, the rule ensures we are not manipulating others to meet our own goals. We allow them to make their own decisions based on the truth rather than on manufactured information. Thus, the rule, "do not cheat," is a valid moral rule.

The reader is forgiven for grumbling about arriving at this conclusion after a mind bending and esoteric process. That complaint may be true, but it's useful to remember the "do not cheat" rule is almost universal among cultures and religions. Cheating is not morally permitted in the major religions and it's not easy to find a culture where cheating is considered morally permissible. Therefore, the rule of not cheating is valid under Kantian ethics and also valid under other duty based ethical systems. In other words, most everyone considers cheating unethical. The upshot is that if I choose to act on my portfolio pumping plans, I will be acting unethically.

Right Action: Stay Calm and Carry on Ethically

An hour or so after I instructed my research analyst to put in the buy orders for the handful of illiquid Hong Kong stocks, he returned, closed the door to my office, and sat down. I surmised from his anguished face he was in deep conflict about carrying out my instructions. There was a fear of offending me, his immediate boss, and then there was the moral uneasiness of doing something wrong. As I suggested in Chapter 2, when you feel morally queasy about doing an act, pay attention because there usually is a well-grounded, rational reason for that feeling. Intuition after all, emerges from a split-second decision that comes out of experience and reason. It was clear the research analyst had rehearsed what he was about to say, which was, he had not put in the orders. Window dressing was unnecessary, he was sure we would do better the next year through our own legitimate efforts. His earnestness and concern moved me (not to tears as per Kant). I canceled the Hong Kong orders and foreswore window dressing. The next year, the fund did perform much better.

Lesson learned: surround yourself with good people, listen to them especially if you know they have your best interest at heart, and do not allow the pressures of the job to break your moral compass.

Notes

1. G. Hu, R. D. McLean, J. Pontiff, and Q. Wang, "The Year-End Trading Activities of Institutional Investors: Evidence from Daily Trades." *Review of Financial Studies*, Vol. 27 (2014), 1593–1614.
2. M. Carhart, R. Kaniel, D. Musto, and A. Reed, "Leaning for the Tape: Evidence of Gaming Behavior in Equity Mutual Funds." *Journal of Finance*, Vol. 57 (2002), 661–693.
3. I. Ben-David, F. Franzoni, A. Landier, and R. Moussawi, "Do Hedge Funds Manipulate Stock Prices?" *Journal of Finance* (2013). Advance Access published. http://doi.org/10.1111/jofi.12062.
4. Karl Jaspers, *Kant* (Orlando, FL: Harcourt Brace & Company, 1957), 4.
5. Roger Scruton, *Kant* (Oxford, UK: Oxford University Press, 1982), 2–8.
6. Ibid.
7. In the Marvel Universe, the defining quality of adamantium is its practical indestructibility. In Marvel Comics adamantium makes up the skeleton and claws of Wolverine and is part of the material that makes up the shell of Ultron. It's a fictional metal but used as a metaphor here to mean unyielding. See https://www.marvel.com/items/adamantium.

CHAPTER 4

Mutual Fund Fun Case Study

THE STORY: QUICK MONEY AT OTHERS' EXPENSE

At some point midway through my tenure as senior portfolio manager of the Fund, there occurred a period of a few months when fund performance noticeably lagged its peers. (This unwanted condition immediately triggers the archetypal stress nightmares where you go into class, forget you have an exam, and freak out from being totally unprepared.) Using our portfolio models my team determined the performance should not have been so poor relative to others in our fund's peer group. Upon further investigation, we discovered large amounts of money were trading in and out of the Fund within 24 to 48 hours. The people doing these trades were "time zone arbitraging" the fund.

The fame of the Fund pretty much skyrocketed after a spectacular performance in 1993 when returns came in at a stunning 87% for the year. Everyone wanted to buy into the Fund, but it was for the most part, closed to new investors. Taking in more money could have a poor effect on performance. At that time, the Asian ex-Japan stock markets were not large and liquid like the U.S. markets. It would have taken some time

Supplementary Information The online version contains supplementary material available at https://doi.org/10.1007/978-3-031-34401-5_4.

K. Tan Bhala, *Ethics in Finance*,
https://doi.org/10.1007/978-3-031-34401-5_4

to put the new funds to work. If the Fund had a say, 25% increase in assets in the space of a week, which was very likely considering the popularity stemming from its performance, the Fund would have excessively high cash levels. The high cash percentage in the portfolio would depress performance if markets moved up. The Company had a fiduciary responsibility to ensure the interests of its existing shareholders were primary and the Company shouldered this responsibility seriously.

Mutual funds comprise a portfolio of stocks, bought and sold daily. As such, the price of each stock in the portfolio affects the price of the mutual fund. The valuation of a mutual fund is known as the Net Asset Value or NAV. The price of a mutual fund shown to the public daily is actually the NAV of the fund. This NAV is calculated at the end of the trading day of the relevant markets. Asian markets based in Asia are twelve hours ahead of the U.S. because of time zone differences. Those in the know and out to make a quick return, can make use of this time difference when trading in Asian equity funds such as the Fund.

Trading in and Out in 24 Hours

While new shareholders were closed from the Fund, existing shareholders could still trade some of their shares in and out of the Fund. Among the thousands of shareholders of the Fund were a few who owned large amounts of fund shares. A handful of these shareholders would take advantage of the time zone difference to make fast returns, at the expense of the other shareholders.

In times of stress and volatility, the Asian markets tend to follow the movements of the U.S. markets. For example, if the Labor Department released an unexpectedly good employment figure, then the U.S. market could rise sharply. Let's say this event happens on Tuesday in the U.S. and the markets close up 3%. As the Asian markets are 12 hours ahead of the U.S., they would already have closed before the U.S. market even opened on Tuesday. Asian markets open trading for Wednesday a few hours after the U.S. closes on Tuesday. If there is a strong correlation in market movements, then someone can buy the Fund just before the market closes on Tuesday in the U.S., expecting to profit from a sharp increase in the NAV of the Fund the next day because Asian markets also move up strongly. This same person sells the Fund on Wednesday after markets increase sharply, making a nice trading profit in the space of 24 hours.

During a period of particularly high volatility in the markets, a high-net-worth client of the Company did just that. This client was not just rich, he also was powerful and famous. He owned at least $100 million worth of various funds of the Company. He would buy millions of dollars worth of shares in the Fund on a Tuesday and then sell the same number of shares on Wednesday with a chunky profit as Asian markets rose in tandem, at greater multiples, with U.S. markets.

A Drag on Performance

Managing a fund with this type of quick inflow and outflow of funds is frustrating for any portfolio manager who cares about performance (which is all of them). The large inflow of funds occurs when the market is moving up. This means the fund has a larger than normal cash position, which acts as a drag on performance. The money is then taken out the next day when the market will likely suffer a sharp correction after rising sharply. Consequently, the cash level sinks leaving less cash to cushion a fall in market prices. In sum, fund performance suffers and existing shareholders are disadvantaged.

The pressure to perform is constant for any portfolio manager. The lack of control of performance during this period when clients were time zone arbitraging the fund frustrated the team and after a few months I was unable and unwilling to tolerate the situation anymore. I walked into the office of the marketing director and beseeched him to first, warn the client that time zone arbitraging the fund was not acceptable. Second, if the behavior continued, the client would then be informed he would not be able to buy back into the fund once he had sold any of its shares. This ultimatum was bold because it could cause the client to take such umbrage, he might pull all his money out of every fund of the Company in which he was invested. I was expecting the marketing manager to kick me out of his office for suggesting this profit unfriendly solution. He listened to my complaint and my reasoning about how bad it was for all shareholders if one or two shareholders practice time zone arbitrage for the sake of self-enrichment. To my surprise, he decided to discuss the situation with the Fund's Board.

The matter was resolved rather quickly, again to my surprise. The Board, in agreement with the marketing team, decided to put in a rule that no shareholder could buy back into a fund within a month of selling the shares of that same fund. In other words, short-term trading of a fund was forbidden. This solution was far less incendiary than the one I suggested, and much more practical. (Perhaps I had let my stressed-out emotions overrule my rational faculties.) The rule was installed and all financial consultants informed clients of this new development. In particular, the financial consultant of the time zone arbitraging client informed his client of the recent rule. There was much moaning and grumbling. Eventually, the client placed additional money into another Asian fund of a different fund group, which allowed short-term trading. I guess my fund lost that extra money, but performance did not get dragged down, my teeth finally unclenched, and the Fund's shareholders were well served from a fiduciary sense.

Ethics Issues: Duty and Fairness

There are two ethics issues in this case. One has to do with fulfilling a fiduciary duty. The other has to do with justice and fairness over the distribution of rewards and burdens. What is not an ethics issue is my distress caused by a loss of control of fund performance. Portfolio manager stress is a mere side effect of the moral problem. Few will have much sympathy for sleepless nights of well-paid finance professionals. Nor is the moral problem the profits lost by the fund management company as a consequence of aggrieved shareholders pulling their money out of funds managed by the company. That event is a possible negative result of right action and often, a ferocious hindrance to choosing the right action. A review of the facts in this case reveals three points. First, a handful of motivated shareholders make use of a 14-hour time difference between markets to trade in and out of the fund, within a day, in order to generate profits for themselves. Second, this trading causes the performance of the fund to suffer because the fund gets a large cash inflow when markets are rising and an equally large cash outflow when the markets are falling. Third, this performance drag harms other shareholders of the fund who don't participate in such short-term trading practices. Suppose Z, a regular, non-arbitrageur shareholder sells the fund on the same day the performance is hit by a large cash inflow. Z will get a worse price than if time zone arbitrageurs had not put substantial money into the fund. In sum, the ethics issue is about fairness. Is it fair that a few (time zone arbitraging shareholders) benefit at the expense of the many (the rest of the shareholders)?

The other ethics issue is hinted at by my previous observation above—the fund management company is likely to lose revenues from time zone arbitraging clients if these clients are prevented from short-term trading. This possible result should not affect the choice of the right course of action. But we live in a business environment still largely driven by neo-liberal economics where profit maximization is sovereign, and monetary loss frequently informs the choice of actions. Should the company place profits before duty to the people who trust it will act in their interest? It soon becomes clear the second ethics issue is what the fund management company is obliged to do in this situation.

In sum the two ethics issues to resolve are:

1. Should shareholders be allowed to do two-day trading in a mutual fund in order to time zone arbitrage?
2. Should a few shareholders be allowed to time zone arbitrage because they hold large positions in the fund or have some other positions of privilege?

ETHICS ANALYSIS: WHAT WOULD SOCRATES DO?

Fiduciary Duty

A fund management company is a fiduciary, which means the company is responsible for managing and caring for the money entrusted to it by a group of people. According to deontological theory, fiduciary duty is a moral principle we are obliged to obey. Deontology concerns the moral duties that apply to moral agents, i.e., us. Accordingly, there are acts we are obliged to perform or to refrain from performing to comply with such duties. Two actors interact in a fiduciary relationship: the principal (the shareholder of the fund) and the agent (the fund management company). A fiduciary duty is embodied in a relationship of trust, where the agent owes allegiance, obedience, and fidelity to the principal.[1] The significant point about fiduciaries is they have a duty to the people for whom they act as fiduciaries. Fiduciary duty is defined as the duty of an agent to act in the best interest of the principal (the one who has entrusted the fiduciary with some asset) even at the expense of the agent. In other words, the fund management company has a fiduciary duty to act in the best interest of the fund's shareholders. The best interest of the shareholders, in this particular case, is served if no short-term time zone arbitraging trades are done, even if a few shareholders benefit. This duty answers the question of whether the company can accommodate those few shareholders because if it does not, there is a possibility they may depart the fund. The answer is no, the company cannot accommodate those few shareholders to prevent a possible decline in revenues the fund management company may incur. The company has to uphold its fiduciary duty to all shareholders at its own expense.

Justice as Fair Treatment

The second ethics issue is whether it is fair to allow some shareholders the privilege of two-day trading to keep them happy and therefore, invested in the fund. To answer questions of fairness, we usually reach for theories of justice. The definition of justice is to give each person her due, treating equals equally and unequals unequally. Aristotle, with his usual genius, wrote this definition and to this day, most agree with his characterization of the term. There are five types of justice: (1) distributive justice, (2) retributive justice, (3) compensatory justice, (4) procedural justice, and (5) commutative justice. Distributive justice concerns the distribution of benefits and burdens, so that everyone receives her fair due. The area of discussion focuses on what is considered fair distribution. Should the rich and the powerful receive a greater proportion of benefits? Or should all be treated equally? Retributive justice is meted out to balance an injustice. Someone who breaks the law or harms another is punished because the moral imbalance must be corrected. The punishment given out is retributive justice. Compensatory justice requires repaying someone for a past injustice or making good harm suffered in the past. Our innate sense of fairness insists on fair compensation for someone who is injured by another who caused the injury. This type of justice may be and often is given through monetary compensation. Procedural justice is about fair decision procedures, practices, or agreements. It concerns the system of justice which involves processes that must be fair and unbiased to ensure fair treatment for those who use the justice system. Commutative justice is relevant whenever there is a transaction. Therefore, it usually is the applicable type of justice in finance and business. Commutative justice refers to fairness in exchange of goods and services. Sellers are expected to set fair prices for their goods and avoid price gouging. This form of justice requires full informational disclosure to both buyer and seller. Each must enter the transaction freely and without coercion. Buyer and seller should see some benefit from the transaction. Not all these modes of justice are applicable to our case.

The relevant forms of justice relevant in this case are types (1) and (5): distributive justice and commutative justice. The question of fair distribution of benefits and burdens in a mutual fund can be put in this way: should all shareholders be treated equally or should the richest/most powerful/most famous/most well-connected (choose the distinguishing factor or even apply all of them) shareholders be given privileges not available to those who hold a small number of shares? From an intuitive or innate sense of fairness, most people would have the gut reaction that all shareholders should be treated equally. A few others, like Thrasymachus in Plato's dialogue, *The Republic*, will argue that justice is nothing but the advantage of the stronger (338c). Thrasymachus argues it is just (by nature) for the strong to rule over the weak. Little is known about the man who held this view, just that he was a sophist who became famous in Athens during the fifth century B.C.E. Thrasymachus' celebrity status comes from Plato casting him as an ambivalent character who is a foil in his *Republic*, refuting Socrates' claim that justice is good. Thrasymachus is the spokesperson for a cynical realism that contends might (or its modern equivalent, money) is right. This view aligns with the attitude of the Athenians when they landed in Melos in the fifth century B.C.E. and demanded the Melians become a tribute state to the Athenian Empire. Just like Thrasymachus, who thought might is right, the Athenians believed they had a right to rule and to invade because of their military strength. Thus, from this dialogue with the Melians emerges the celebrated saying, "the strong do what they can and the weak suffer what they must."[2] This anti-social view is then taken up and fully elaborated by Machiavelli in his book, *The Prince*.

To finish the story in the *Republic*, Socrates' response to Thrasymachus' challenge is that it is in everyone's interest to act justly because we live in a human community and our happiness comes from being part of this community. Tyrants are rarely happy it seems. Behaving unjustly, which involves disregarding another's good, is incompatible with being unified with others and with our own happiness.

With all this in mind and getting back to our case, we already have an intuitive reaction based on our innate sense of fairness that all shareholders should be treated equally. While it is unwise to follow just our feelings when making moral choices, we can back this particular intuition with a reasoned argument for this position. Individuals buy into the fund with the reasonable expectation that every shareholder will be treated equally. In this sense, every shareholder bears the same attributable benefits as well as burdens. Everyone is charged the same percentage of fees, is bound by the same rules of the fund, and is due the same returns on the fund. The obligations of both the fund management company and the shareholders are disclosed in the fund prospectus. Indeed, shareholders trust there is full disclosure on the part of the fund management company. Commutative justice, the form of justice that covers transactions, demands transparency on the part of both seller and buyer.

If the fund management company decides to treat shareholders unequally, then it should say so openly and with full transparency so shareholders know what they are buying. However, no such disclosure exists stating the unequal treatment of shareholders. Therefore, privileging rich shareholders who hold many shares by allowing them to engage in short-term trading is unfair from a commutative justice approach. When shareholders discover the unequal treatment, small shareholders will sell their shares, and avoid the funds managed by the offending fund management company. In turn, the revenues of the company will fall due to lower assets under management. Mutual fund companies cannot depend merely on the patronage of wealthy customers who buy large holdings in the fund. In this matter, Socrates was right, we live in a human community. In the community of mutual fund shareholders, we depend on others to act in a just manner, in order for the proper functioning of the community. From a utilitarian point of view, the action of not treating shareholders equally is also unethical because the outcomes are unfavorable both to the company (a fall in revenues and in customer trust) and individual clients (loss of choice in mutual funds). Thus, from a justice perspective and a utilitarian approach, treating shareholders unequally by allowing some to trade intraday because they have a particular perceived privileged position, fails the ethics test.

Right Action: Engage in Transparency and Fairness

If allowing short-term trading for the sake of time zone arbitraging is wrong, then logically, the fund management company should stop this activity and put in rules that would prevent the future activity of the same sort. Happily, in this case, the ethical actions that needed to be taken, were taken. Optimally, this right action should be done in a transparent and fair way. The new rules must be highlighted, especially to past traders. Clear and comprehensible reasons should be given for not allowing this type of trading. A majority of people will be persuaded by ethical reasoning and regardless if this belief is idealistic and empirically wrong (which it's not), we still have an ethical duty to be transparent.

NOTES

1. Seven Pillars Institute, "The Ethics of Executive Compensation: A Matter of Duty" (June 15, 2015). https://sevenpillarsinstitute.org/the-ethics-of-executive-compensation-a-matter-of-duty/. Accessed February 9, 2020.
2. Thucydides, *History of the Peloponnesian War*, trans. Richard Crawley (London: J.M. Dent E.P. Dutton, 1910).

CHAPTER 5

High Finance Gender Inequity Case Study

The Story: An Inner Sanctum for Men Only

I don't mean to imply by the title of this case study that gender inequity occurs only in high finance, by which I mean Wall Street type finance. This would be far from reality. Of the instances of overt gender inequity I have experienced over my career in finance, I recount the story behind this case study because it is a little more unusual and entertaining in its details, if somewhat depressing upon deeper reflection.

By the time this story takes place, I had already risen to the position of Managing Director (MD) of the asset management company (the Company) I worked at, one of the approximately 10% of women MDs in the group. The Company was a division of a large multinational financial institution that boasted about 60,000 employees. I was one of two female senior portfolio managers in the Company that employed roughly 40–60 senior portfolio managers. Undoubtedly the ratio of senior-level women to men was abominable both at group and company levels. Regrettably, appreciable change in the number of women in senior management roles has not occurred in financial services. In 2021 women made up a mere

Supplementary Information The online version contains supplementary material available at https://doi.org/10.1007/978-3-031-34401-5_5.

23.8% of investment bankers.[1] They earned 90 cents for every dollar earned by men. A Catalyst study reports that women account for less than a quarter (21.9%) of senior leadership roles within financial services firms.[2] In private equity, women comprise only 9% of senior executives and only 18% of total employees.[3] In a CNBC/LinkedIn survey of women and men in financial services across in the U.S., nearly two-thirds of women polled say females are less likely than males to reach leadership roles.[4] Only 40% of women but 75% of men agree that genders working at the same level are paid equally at their companies.[5] About a third of men and women say an unsupportive or biased corporate culture is the biggest obstacle preventing women from advancing.[6] According to a McKinsey report, gender diversity in banking reflects the reality in financial services overall, with an even split between men and women at entry level that declines with each rung up the ladder. Women make up 53% of the entry-level banking workforce but less than one-third at the SVP and C-suite levels.[7]

Blatant hostility toward women has become less common as Wall Street firms have responded to sex discrimination suits and the #MeToo movement. Yet, the problem persists. The larger causes of gender discrimination on Wall Street are more subtle. Most senior managers are aware of how they are supposed to behave toward women in the workplace, but a lot of inequalities arise because of managerial discretion.[8] According to Louis Marie Roth, managerial discretion is a problem because those in power tend to favor others like themselves. The industry is dominated by white men, many of whom have discretionary power over other workers. On Wall Street, this means the majority of managers favor white men when they allocate opportunities and accounts. They may not deliberately overlook women, but they tend to gravitate toward men—giving them the pick of deals. This sort of discrimination does not end just in the workplace and with the assignment of the best work. Readers may not be surprised to discover that women are barred from networking opportunities outside the workplace. Take company holiday parties for instance.

My first six months at the Company were busy and I was energized by the work. I loved my job and my team, and I liked the Company. So far, so good, I thought. Soon enough, the holiday season arrived. The Company always hosted a lavish holiday party for its staff (it was the roaring nineties after all), reserving a large ballroom at one of the best hotels in town. There was gourmet food—shrimp cocktails, smoked salmon, charcuterie boards, roast beef, honeyed ham, Peking duck, luscious cakes, and delicate desserts. The wines, white, red and bubbly, flowed generously. The beer was premium. A pop music band of some renown entertained. I stepped into the festooned ballroom and was impressed by the Company's generosity and thoughtfulness in providing this extravagant end-of-year party for its employees. My husband and I joined a group of colleagues, enjoying the convivial company and warming fare. Over the course of our celebrations, I noticed men steadily trickling toward a room at the back of the ballroom. Each would open the heavy wooden door and enter the room, making sure to close the door behind him. A few would look back into the ballroom quickly, before disappearing into the back room. These movements piqued my interest and I walked toward the door wondering what I was missing. (Admittedly, at that time I was young enough to suffer from FOMO.[9]) As I approached the door and reached for the handle, a man in a dark green uniform, a host from the hotel, I guessed, quietly appeared in front of me and asked if he could help.

"Just wanted to check out the room inside and find out what's happening in there." I said casually, expecting him to open the door for me with a welcoming smile. But no!

"I'm sorry ma'am but I'm afraid entry is by invitation only" he said. I was nonplussed. What could that inner room be concealing?

"What's happening in there?" I asked.

"There's food and wine as well." The man in the green uniform answered with some embarrassed formality.

"Oh, really? Who's in there?" I asked.

"The president of the Company is in there with his guests," he replied.

Ah, light bulbs switch on. The top brass and their buddies go in there. That's the Inner Sanctum.

I later found out from other Inner Sanctum outcasts that this event happened every year. At the annual Company holiday party there was always a room, nearly always the same room, an Inner Sanctum, where senior-level male executives at the Company gathered and socialized. I must have been more piqued than annoyed at that point because my training as an equity analyst tripped in. Questions like, how does one wrangle an invitation? When did this gathering start? What do they do in the Inner Sanctum? Is there on average, higher remuneration for the Inner Sanctum group than for the excluded? I knew some of the men who were members of this exclusive group. At one holiday party a few years later, a well-respected senior portfolio manager who worked in the office next to mine, was walking by as I chatted with friends. He stopped to say a quick hello and breezily continued on his way to the Inner Sanctum. If he thought there was anything wrong with an exclusive all-male group networking within an organization's holiday party, he showed no sign of his disquiet. Indeed, if any men in the Inner Sanctum were not comfortable with the arrangement, they did not speak up nor try to change the system, as far as I knew. I worked at the Company for a decade. Although annual holiday parties remained a constant, I was never invited into the Inner Sanctum.

ETHICS ISSUES: GENDER EXCLUSION, GENDER DISCRIMINATION

The key ethics issue is gender discrimination, which in this case entails the exclusion of a person from a group based on her gender. Job discrimination is to withhold a job from a person because of gender/race/religion/sexual identity/age. In this case, we observe discrimination *on* the job because a person is not invited to a certain work-related group because of her gender. Entering this group is likely to open up new contacts and job enhancing possibilities. Discrimination in any of its forms (e.g., sex, race, religion, age) is unethical under every ethical system of thought out there today. Focusing just on gender discrimination, I explain how this practice is unethical when evaluated through the lenses of (1) justice theory, (2) rights theory, (3) duty-based ethics, (4) natural law theory, (5) utilitarianism and, (6) feminist ethics. The upshot at the end of this comprehensive ethics analysis is there simply is no moral justification for gender discrimination.

ETHICS ANALYSIS: ALL THEORIES SAY GENDER DISCRIMINATION IS WRONG

Justice as Fairness

We discussed a theory of justice in Chapter 4 and defined justice as giving each person her due, treating equals equally, and unequals unequally. Based on this definition, to leave women out from the Inner Sanctum is unethical because a female vice president of the Company, is equal in organizational position and in human dignity to a male vice president. If the Inner Sanctum was reserved for vice presidents and above, then surely there should have been some women in the room. Chapter 4 shone a light on Aristotle's theory of justice, but in this chapter, the focus falls on John Rawls' distributive justice. John Rawls (1921–2002) developed a splendid theory of justice usually called "Justice as Fairness." The system is well regarded and has been applied in actual functioning societies. The theory of justice Rawls developed tackles the question of how rights and duties, benefits and burdens, are to be fairly distributed between members of a society. The principles Rawls elucidated also are applicable at a micro level to the distribution of rewards and work in an organization. Rawls laid out two renowned principles of justice and the one relevant to this case is the equality of opportunity principle: positions and offices should be open to all under conditions of fair equality of opportunity. This principle calls for equal access to all positions and offices. Thus, a person cannot be discriminated against getting a job because she is a woman. Nor should a person be excluded from company networking groups that may open more opportunities in terms of lucrative deals, promotions, and jobs, because she is a woman. Blocking access to opportunities also blocks the advancement of women and therefore, obstructs equality of opportunity.

Rights and Kantian Ethics

The oldest basis of human rights or the justifiable moral claims to which humans are entitled by virtue of being human, arise from religion. God confers inviolable rights to humans. These God-given rights, such as the right to freedom, and equal treatment are called natural rights. In the secular versions of human rights, the notion emerges from Kant's moral theory. If the reader recalls from Chapter 3, in our detailed discussion of Kantian duty-based ethics, Kant's second formulation of the categorical imperative states, "Act so that you treat humanity, whether in your own person or in that of another, always as an end and never as a means only."[10] This second formulation means we must respect human beings as ends in themselves because every human being has dignity and is therefore, deserving of respect. Respect for people means fair and equal treatment irrespective of gender. Kant writes, "There is nothing more sacred in the wide world than the rights of others. They are inviolable."[11] A Kantian ethics insists that rights cannot be violated simply for the sake of promoting desirable ends, whether for oneself, or others. In this case, there is no moral justification according to Kantian ethics, for women to be excluded from the Inner Sanctum simply because male vice presidents and higher, desire a space where only men can hang out and do "guy" things (presumably) during company holiday parties.

Some regard rights as indispensable for countering gender discrimination. Supporters point to the burgeoning global feminist movement inspired by the slogan, "Women's rights are human rights." This slogan emerged from a grassroots activist movement and indicates a vision that is ethical. The statement has a good claim to expressing a general consensus of feminists worldwide.

Natural Law Theory

Natural law theory started with, well, who else—the Greeks, and in particular, the Stoics. A vital element in natural law theory is the concept of *telos*, ancient Greek meaning purpose. The Greeks believed everything in nature has a purpose. The world has a rational natural order and part of that order requires values and purpose to be built into its very nature. Rationality or *logos* underlies everything. In short, the world is an orderly, rational system, with each thing having its own proper place and servicing its own special purpose. Christian thinkers were drawn to this natural law system of thought but added God into the mix. Thus, values and purposes are conceived as part of God's plan. St. Thomas Aquinas (1225–1274), arguably the most illustrious and brilliant of thinkers in the medieval period of philosophy, also stands as the greatest natural law theorist. While some may disagree with the statement that Thomas is the greatest philosopher of all time, few would dispute his status as the greatest philosopher for the two thousand years between Aristotle and Descartes. He represents the medieval mind par excellence. While Thomas is the star moral theologian of the Catholic Church, his philosophical works are relevant today for non-believers because natural law is based on reason and develops out of ancient Greek thought.

For Thomas, God created the world, establishing a sense of order and purpose that reflects their will. If everything is created for a purpose, then human reason, in examining the purpose, is able to judge how to act in order to conform to that purpose. In sum, God gives everyone reason in order to discover moral truth. Everyone means not just Christians, but also non-believers. If one is human, one has the rational capacity to figure out what is right and what is wrong. The "natural laws" that specify what we should do are laws of reason, which we are able to grasp because God has given us the power to understand them. Natural law theory endorses the idea the right thing to do is whatever action has the best reasons backing it up. The religious believer does not have special access to moral truth. The believer and the non-believer are in the same position. God gives everyone the ability to listen to reason and follow its directives. Even though they may disagree about religion, believers and non-believers inhabit the same moral universe.

And in this universe, the prime moral directive is, in short, do good and avoid evil. In Thomas' words, the fundamental principle of natural law states "good is to be done and pursued, and evil is to be avoided (STIaIIae 94, 2)."[12] All other precepts of natural law are rooted in this fundamental notion. Before the reader stands aghast at the mention of evil, let me propose that evil in natural law theory is not necessarily the evil we usually associate with Satan, Hell, and the Omen (Parts I-III). For Thomas, evil is the absence of the good. If a person does not act according to the good in her, she is lacking in goodness in that particular act. In modern secular parlance, the fundamental principle of natural law becomes, "do good, avoid harm." Now, let's engage in some casuistry, a fancy word to be sure. Casuistry means to apply general principles of natural law to specific cases. The word is now used generally for any system that starts with fixed principles and then applies them logically to individual situations.

Applying the primary natural law principle to this case, we find not allowing women into the Inner Sanctum does not (1) do good; nor does the action (2) avoid harm. To do good would be to help women succeed and achieve their potential by allowing them a place at the table. Don't exclude women so as to enjoy an evening with your fellow men, smoking cigars (yes, they did that in the Inner Sanctum) and drinking whiskey (the alcoholic choice for real men?). Discriminating against women just because of gender is harmful in all sorts of ways to women. The harm inflicted depends on the situation in which the discrimination takes place. In the workplace, discriminating against women hinders their career progress, retards realization of their full capabilities, and reduces the economic gains which they have a right to earn.

Utilitarianism

Utilitarianism is an ethical theory that evaluates the rightness of an action according to the resulting consequences of that action.[13] The motives of the act are not taken into account. How the act is done, or the character of the actor also does not matter. To determine if the act is ethical or not ethical requires knowledge of the consequences or outcomes of the act. For this reason, utilitarianism is a sub-genre of ethics known as consequentialism. Classical utilitarianism possesses these three principles:

1. Judge actions to be right or wrong solely on the consequences of the actions
2. Assess consequences by the amount of happiness or unhappiness created
3. Each person's happiness counts the same

The English philosopher, Jeremy Bentham (1748–1832) was the first to set out the theory of utilitarianism. Bentham, a philosopher, economist, and legal reformer wrote the famous line, "the greatest happiness of the greatest number," which became the principle of utilitarianism. For Bentham, happiness is simply measured by the amount of pleasure attained and pain avoided. The principle can be reformulated as "the greatest good for the greatest number." Bentham wanted to develop a scientific method of ethics. Like many current financial academics, Bentham was seduced by the belief that any quantitative system is also objective and therefore, reliably accurate. The quantitative aspect of the utilitarian theory involves counting the numbers as well as obtaining a measure of the amount of happiness or pleasure attained. If the final balance is more pleasure than pain, then the act should be done. If the final balance is more pain than pleasure, then the act should not be done. This focus on measuring happiness shows the depth of Bentham's insistence on ethics as a quantitative analysis of pleasure and pain. The whole calculus is a matter of numbers derived from hard data. This notion of quantitative and scientific credibility largely explains why utilitarianism, in its various forms, continues to command the attention of philosophers and economists. The utilitarian framework is one of the most widespread and influential of ethical theories. Bentham would be quite pleased about the impact of a system he championed, as he watches, seated on his ornate mahogany chair, within the glass-fronted case, that rests not in the least bit creepily at all, at University College London, England.[14]

Bentham would likely agree with the results of the proceeding evaluation using utilitarianism for our particular case. Exclusion of women from the Inner Sanctum produces the following bad consequences:

1. Women feel excluded, hurt, and undervalued versus men.
2. As a result of (1) above, some women could have less motivation at work.
3. The company loses the loyalty of women, some may be talented and may contribute positively to the company.
4. Women lose the ability to network at an important work-related social event. They may then miss opportunities to work on big, profitable deals, that usually lead to promotions and salary increases.
5. By excluding women so visibly, the rest of the company will not take seriously the anti-discrimination policies and the gender sensitivity training the company provides. Employees will view these efforts as mere public relations and as an activity to impede lawsuits. The exclusion of women encourages both overt and implicit discrimination.
6. If this type of behavior becomes public, the company's reputation could suffer.

The good outcomes of this discriminatory act are:

1. Men get to enjoy a night with their fellow men, chatting perhaps about women, and speaking in politically insensitive ways generally unacceptable in progressive society.
2. Some men may delight in the feeling of (false) exclusivity and belonging to a privileged group, not just for a night, but the feeling may continue to uplift them through the year.

In evaluating the amount of the good versus bad consequences of excluding women from the Inner Sanctum, reasonable minds will agree the bad outcomes outweigh the good ones. The bad outcomes affect the entire company, because there will be a loss of talent, morale, possibly revenues, and finally organizational reputation. The minority (we hope) of men, vice president and above, whose loyalty to the company is strengthened by being included in the Inner Sanctum, is not outweighed by the majority of women whose morale and loyalty to the firm decline.

Feminist Ethics

The reader may be surprised, or not, to hear that for much of the history of Western ethics, the dominant view in the tradition held that women's moral worth was less than that of men. Feminist ethics came about only in the 1980s. Western moral philosophy's disregard for women's interests has often been justified by denying that women are full moral agents. Basing ethical theory on a model of human nature that reflects men's distinctive experiences and values is problematic most obviously because it valorizes the ethical perspectives of only one segment of the population. Feminist ethics believes it is necessary to demonstrate that women's claims to moral concern are equal to men's. Feminist ethical theory is often equated with the ethics of care but in fact the only orthodoxy in feminist ethical theory is its broad commitment to eliminating male bias. [15,16]

One feminist response in ethics is the notion of "capabilities." This approach was pioneered by Amartya Sen as an alternative to utilitarianism. Sen's "capabilities approach" is the central theoretical framework behind the annual Human Development Reports, which since 1990, the United Nations Development Program (UNDP) produces. The UNDP designed its Human Development Index and Gender-Related Development Index in consultation with Sen. Martha Nussbaum developed the concept further, applying an Aristotelian framework to capabilities and functionings in critical conversation with Sen's approach. Nussbaum proposes capabilities as a universal standard for measuring people's quality of life. We assess this quality by how well a society enables women to develop and realize their distinctively human capabilities. Sen focuses his work on understanding the condition of girls and women in development as well as their crucial role as agents in that process. Sen provides distinctive insights for ethical analyses of gender discrimination as his capability approach argues all human beings should have an equality of basic capability. This argument provides a moral justification for attending to and confronting discrimination against women in various aspects of life. Though Sen designed his capabilities framework to address problems of developing countries, it also offers lessons for studying the condition of women in high-income societies.

Sen's insights are a resource for analyzing discrimination against women and for promoting their well-being and moral agency. [17] What is important normatively for a woman's well-being is what she is able to do or to be, not just what possessions or income she holds. The activities women actually accomplish, such as being well nourished and engaging in paid work, are called functionings. Having adequate income is itself one important functioning because it gives people access to basic goods and services and it conveys one's social status. The bundle, or choice, of the functionings that a person can select entails his or her capability set. To illustrate, let's apply the capabilities framework to our case study. A woman has access to high-level executives in the C suite because of family or friend connections. She chooses not to avail herself of this access because she prefers to live a simple, introvert way of life. Yet, this woman has the capability to network. However, a woman without access because she lacks family or friend connections and is blocked by gender discrimination from establishing such access, does not have the capability to network. Neither the well-connected person nor the poorly connected person has the functioning of network access, but the former enjoys a kind of freedom that the latter does not. Sen asserts that the emphasis on capability and functionings focuses on those aspects of human development and well-being we value. Society's commitment to treating its citizens as moral equals is best expressed in terms of establishing equality of capabilities. Clearly, gender discrimination reduces the equality of capabilities.

RIGHT ACTION: STAND UP FOR WOMEN'S RIGHTS

I regret not speaking up against the exclusion of women from the Inner Sanctum. I was a Managing Director who managed one of the most popular and successful funds in the Company, which gave me a little more clout than the average female employee. Unfortunately, at that time in history, gender discrimination was not as badly thought of as it is now. The #MeToo movement has thankfully elevated the issue to the forefront of society's collective consciousness. Lane and Percy in their 2003 research on gender discrimination in the nursing profession conclude that not least among the reasons why female career development disadvantage continues to exist is quite simply that managers do not believe there is anything morally or ethically unacceptable in this discriminatory behavior.[18] Even now with greater racial and gender sensitivity, paradoxically, there also is an apparent increase in racism and sexism. The 2019 occupant of the White House, through discriminatory rhetoric and unbecoming behavior on gender and race issues, gave cover and encouragement to these deleterious trends. I am hopeful the new occupant of the White House will reverse this regrettable regression.

I should have taken my concerns about the Inner Sanctum exclusion of women to my boss, a man, and an invitee to the Inner Sanctum. I may have found it useful to discuss the issue with other women and men who were sympathetic to my view. I could have brought this issue to the human resources diversity division. Among women there is a view that those among us who complain too loudly about gender discrimination, are blackballed from whatever industry we work in. That woman is subsequently labeled a troublemaker who is unable to work well with others. I believe this view to be true to this day. One needs only to observe the depressing spectacle of Christine Blasey Ford's public case against Brett Kavanaugh (now Supreme Court Justice) for sexual assault.[19] In gender discrimination and assault cases, women face a herculean task when they take on powerful men. The capability to enact change and obtain justice increases when women who have suffered discrimination in the same organization band together to make collective complaint. Blasey Ford was a single voice. In contrast, multiple courageous women finally came forward to confront Harvey Weinstein, a formidable Hollywood figure, for sexual assault.[20] He is now convicted and in prison. Many women, 23 to be precise, joined together to complain about Roger Ailes (chairman and CEO of Fox News, Fox Television Stations, and 20th Television) and his sexual harassment of women.[21] In 2016 he was forced to resign from his positions, and he died on May 18, 2017. Until the world is sufficiently changed so a woman can be a lone voice against implicit and explicit gender discrimination in an organization, women standing together have a better chance of stopping such behavior.

NOTES

1. Zippia, Investment Banker Demographics and Statistics in the US. https://www.zippia.com/investment-banker-jobs/demographics/. Accessed April 4, 2023.
2. Catalyst, Women in Financial Services (Quick Take), June 20, 2020. https://www.catalyst.org/research/women-in-financial-services/. Accessed April 4, 2023.
3. Prequin, Prequin Special Report: Women in Alternative Assets (October 2017). https://docs.preqin.com/reports/Preqin-Special-Report-Women-in-Alternative-Assets-October-2017.pdf.
4. Julia Boorstin, "Survey: It's still tough to be a woman on Wall Street – but men don't always notice" CNBC.com, June 26, 2018. Accessed April 14, 2020. https://www.cnbc.com/2018/06/25/surveyon-wall-street-workplace-biases-persist---but-men-dont-see-t.html.
5. *Ibid.*
6. *Ibid.*
7. McKinsey & Company, "Closing the Gender and Race Gaps in North American Financial Services." October 21, 2021. https://www.mckinsey.com/industries/financial-services/our-insights/closing-the-gender-and-race-gaps-in-north-american-financial-services. Accessed April 4, 2023.
8. Louis Marie Roth, "Women on Wall Street: Despite Diversity Measures, Wall Street Remains Vulnerable to Sex Discrimination Charges." *Academy of Management Perspectives*, Vol. 21, Issue 1, February 2007, 35–36.
9. Fear **Of** **M**issing **O**ut.
10. Kara Tan Bhala, Warren Yeh and Raj Bhala, *International Investment Management: Theory, Ethics and Practice* (London, UK: Routledge, 2016), 288–289.
11. *Ibid.*
12. Peter Kreeft, *Summa of the Summa*, (San Francisco, CA: Ignatius Press, 1990), 515.
13. Kara Tan Bhala et al. (2016), 272.
14. After Bentham's death, in accordance with his directions, his body was dissected in the presence of his friends. The skeleton was then reconstructed, supplied with a wax head to replace the original (which had been mummified), dressed in Bentham's own clothes and set upright in a glass fronted case. Both this effigy and the head are preserved in University College London.
15. In response to the charge that modern ethical theory assumes masculine experience as normative, some feminist ethics seeks to take women's experience as a model or point of departure. The ethics of care is well known example of this approach. This theory elaborates a moral perspective postulated to arise from women's characteristic experiences of nurturing

others, especially their experiences of rearing children. Values such as emotional sensitivity and responsiveness should be given ethical priority. The ethics of care has been criticized for, among other flaws, not reflecting the empirical dispositions in women toward empathy and sensitivity but the cultural expectation that women be more empathic and sensitive than men. Another concern is that the ethics of care is insufficiently suspicious of the characteristically feminine moral railing of self-sacrifice.

16. Alison M. Jaggar, "Feminist Ethics," *The Blackwell Guide to Ethical Theory*, 2nd. Edition, eds. Hugh LaFollette and Ingmar Persson (Oxford: Blackwell Publishing, 2013), 433.

17. Douglas A. Hicks, "Gender, Discrimination, and Capability: Insights from Amartya Sen," *The Journal of Religious Ethics*, Vol. 30, Issue 1, Spring 2002, 137–154.

18. Nikala Lane and Nigel F. Piercy, "The Ethics of Discrimination: Organizational Mindsets and Female Employment Disadvantage," *Journal of Business Ethics*, Vol. 44, Issue 4, June 2003, 313–325.

19. Megan Garber, "Christine Blasey Ford Didn't Come Forward in Vain," *The Atlantic*, October 6, 2018. https://www.theatlantic.com/entertainment/archive/2018/10/did-christine-blasey-ford-come-forward-nothing/572380/. Accessed May 19, 2020.

20. BBC News, "Harvey Weinstein timeline: How the scandal unfolded". https://www.bbc.com/news/entertainment-arts-41594672. Accessed May 19, 2020.

21. Manuel Roig-Franzia, Scott Higham, Paul Farhi and Krissah Thompson, "The Fall of Roger Ailes: He made Fox News His 'Locker Room'— And Now Women Are Telling Their Stories." *Washington Post*, July 22, 2016. https://www.washingtonpost.com/lifestyle/style/the-fall-of-roger-ailes-he-made-fox-his-locker-room--and-now-women-are-telling-their-stories/2016/07/22/5eff9024-5014-11e6-aa14-e0c1087f7583_story.html. Accessed May 19, 2020.

CHAPTER 6

Hedge Fund Edge Case Study

THE STORY: PUSHING THE EDGE TO GET AN EDGE

A year after my daughter was born and ten years after I had started the mutual fund at the Company, I stepped off the portfolio management treadmill to spend guilt-free, unconstrained time with her. Corporate America and Political America conspire to make it difficult for women to combine demanding paid work with quality time for children. Something has to give, and sometimes, it's the woman's mental health and the balance of her being. I was fortunate to have the resources to choose less stress and to focus on my daughter. In any case, the time off from paid work also was a good opportunity to pursue further studies in philosophy, and I enrolled in a master's program which eventually led (ahem, ten years later), to a Ph.D. in philosophy. After my daughter started elementary school, I decided to return to work in finance on a part-time basis. A trifling mystery of the universe concerns why I chose to re-enter the industry through a hedge fund, an intense and high-stress segment of asset management.

Supplementary Information The online version contains supplementary material available at https://doi.org/10.1007/978-3-031-34401-5_6.

To understand the reasons for hedge fund manager intensity and drive, we need to talk a little about this method of investment. Hedge funds fall under the category of alternative investments. These investment funds consist of pooled money, managed by professional portfolio managers, but on steroids. In 1949 Australian born Alfred Jones began "hedging" his long-term holdings in a fund he started by selling short other stocks as well as using leverage to increase his returns. Thus, began the first hedge fund. Jones is credited with adding the traditional 20% incentive fee for manager compensation as well as using a partnership structure to reduce individual risk. Investment strategies have changed over time and hedging no longer stands as the distinguishing feature of hedge funds. What has not changed much at all is the fee structure that Jones instituted. Hedge funds generally charge a two percent management fee and a twenty percent performance fee ("two-and-twenty"). Some funds have the temerity to charge a thirty percent performance fee. With falling relative performance and an oversupply of hedge funds, these fees have started to decline just a little. Yet, it is telling that fee structure is the distinctive feature which defines a hedge fund. Otherwise, commentators correctly acknowledge that hedge funds are difficult to characterize. Their investment styles range from macro to micro stock picking, long/short to long only, and arbitrage to quantitative modeling. Using one or more of these techniques, hedge funds invest in nearly all asset classes from fixed income, equities, commodities, currencies, to gold bullion, and oil in tankers. Thus, we cannot define hedge funds by investment style or the type of asset classes in which they invest. We are left with the fee structure as the means of defining a hedge fund. And the fees are incredibly lucrative for the moderately successful hedge fund manager, which makes it even more vital for a hedge fund to outperform in up markets and not lose any capital in down markets. There is much (big money, private islands, named museum wings) at stake.

After a not trivial amount of time off from the finance ecosystem, I stepped right back into this world, through the macho arena of hedge funds. The hedge fund I was employed at was a relatively small one with less than four portfolio managers and 10 or so staff members. On the investment side of the business, I was the only woman. The other woman in the firm worked on accounts and settlements. The fund was owned by a white, middle-aged man (the Owner) who had made his vast wealth on Wall Street and had then put a sizeable portion of it into this hedge fund. He brought his former Wall Street clients into the fund, relying on his investment credibility gained over years. The aim was to grow this fund through outstanding performance and make even more money than he had previously accumulated. The Owner wanted to cultivate a hard charging, aggressive, work-till-you-drop, hyper driven, and performance at all cost, culture. In other words, he aimed to instill a stereotypical hedge fund ethos. He wanted his people to be available 24/7, ensure all information was seized the millisecond after it came out, analyzed, and the necessary follow-up action implemented in rapid time. There would be no holds barred, it seemed, to get actionable information because information is the motherlode. Procuring information before anyone else gets you the winning ticket. If for example, you find out, before anyone else, a company had terrible sales over the last few weeks of the quarter, you can short the stock before investors dump shares in knee-jerk disappointment. Even the idioms of the hedge fund business deal mainly with information:

- Deep dive—analyze all information as deeply as possible. Get all the details of all facets of the company under investigation.
- Granularity—investigate the tiniest details, examine information under a microscope.
- Metrics—a wide variety of data points generated from a multitude of methods to evaluate the performance of a company.
- Data dump—transfer of a big bunch of quantitative information.
- Hungry—those who desire, to the core of their beings, to get high returns and profits and therefore, will toil for information.

In my recent conversations with former hedge fund managers, one talked about how his erstwhile cohorts or "hedgies" are so hungry for new information, whole industries have sprouted up to provide information that give managers an edge. He describes a demonstration from an information provider:

The latest offering is an alt-data product. The information provider takes satellite imagery of all the world's iron ore mines (or some type of extracted resource) and then uses software to create the images of their inventory footprints. These images of the above ground inventory are mapped over and over again and through time-lapse views you are able to see the trend of mineral piles expand and contract. The point is, if you follow their data, you have "first to market" intel on inventory consumption, even before the companies release the figures internally. This is information that can give you an "edge". Similar types of alt-data content have become almost mundane – shopping mall parking lots for instance or credit card data. I mean, if everyone has an edge then no one has an edge.

In the hedge fund fraternity, information is king. Therefore, it is not a surprise to learn of keen, hungry investors who seek non-public, material information—the definition of insider information—because as the former hedge fund manager said, if everyone has an edge, no one has an edge. Insider information gives you the ultimate edge.

Back at my little hedge fund group, the Owner regularly pressed investment staff hard to get information that gave us an edge. I had to make calls daily, sometimes multiple times a day (and night) to portfolio companies, in particular, a company based in China, which was one of the fund's most sizeable position. I would ask the same questions, in different ways and from different angles, but the company would be careful not to divulge non-public information. The Owner would demand we call the company's founder, his wife, and children involved in the business. There was unimaginable pressure on the fund's investment professionals to get information that would give us the edge. The rewards of getting that morsel of information to score a huge return are as seductive to hedge fund managers as the promise of woven gold from hay was to the king in Grimm's *Rumpelstiltskin*. In the fairy tale, that king imprisoned a woman, and threatened to behead her, to get that gold. In the same way, at the hedge fund, the desire to acquire inside information was so immense that one could be seduced into doing harmful acts.

ETHICS ISSUE: INSIDER INFORMATION

The ethics issue is whether to succumb to the temptation to obtain inside information for outsized returns. The phrase "insider trading" includes both legal and illegal conduct. The legal form of insider trading is when corporate insiders (such as officers, directors, and employees) buy and sell stock in their own companies. In the U.S. when corporate insiders trade in their own securities, they must report their trades to the Securities and Exchange Commission (SEC). In this case study, we refer to the other type of insider trading, deemed illegal, defined as the trading of stock of publicly held corporations, in breach of a fiduciary duty or other relationship of trust and confidence, while in possession of material, non-public information about the stock. This sort of trading is an activity founded on asymmetrical information. Those who give such information, or "tippers," the people who use the information to trade the stock, or "tippees," and those who misappropriate such information for stock trading, are all violating insider trading laws. Sections 10b-5 and 14e-3 of the Securities and Exchange Act of 1934 govern U.S. insider trading rules. The key elements to consider when deciding whether an act constitutes insider trading are:

1. The information must be both material and non-public.
2. The trader has violated a fiduciary and/or legal duty to a corporation and its shareholders.
3. The source of the information has a fiduciary and/or legal duty, and the one who trades on this information knows the source is violating the duty.

Most European countries enacted insider trading regulations in the early 1990s, and in 2003, the European Union introduced the Market Abuse Directive (MAD). The Directive prohibits primary and secondary insiders from engaging in the following acts:

1. Using their inside information in conducting a transaction.
2. Disclosing the inside information to a third party.
3. Recommending a transaction to a third party.

After the Global Financial Crisis several high-profile financiers in the U.S. were successfully prosecuted and subsequently imprisoned for insider trading. The most publicized and biggest insider trading cases were the Raj Rajaratnam, Rajat Gupta, and the SAC cases. These prosecutions were carried out to discourage future insider trading activity. Why did prosecutors and regulators feel it necessary to deter this type of trading? Indeed, many free market and market efficiency proponents argue insider trading should not be illegal because the activity actually leads to more efficient price discovery. This argument is economic and uses a utilitarian calculation as support. However, the evaluation takes into account only one aspect of the utility calculation and is therefore, incomplete. On deeper and more reflective analysis, there are a number of sound arguments why insider trading is unethical.

ETHICS ANALYSIS: WHY INSIDER TRADING IS UNETHICAL

Fairness

Insider trading analogizes to a test taker obtaining answers to exam questions because she has connections with the person who set the exam. She pays the exam preparer or uses other means as a bribe for the answers. A salient example which comes instantly comes to mind is the college admission scandal in 2020 which outraged the public.[1] Why were we so outraged? Because we believed it was stunningly unfair how children of wealthy parents could get admitted into elite schools simply because they bribed and paid their way in. These wealthy and covetous parents used their resources to bribe college coaches to admit their offspring into elite colleges based on false athletic credentials. Some parents paid experienced test takers to do the SATs for their children or bribed someone in authority to switch out exams. These parents cheated to get their kids into top-ranked colleges. Humans generally dislike cheating to get ahead because most societies consider the act of cheating to be unfair.

In financial markets, fairness does not require all parties to possess the same information. Markets function well and with credibility when some players have superior information and trade on the information to make profits. However, the information is obtained through work and time spent on analyzing companies and economies. The rewards from superior information obtained through effort give incentives to seek out new information. In other words, fairness is not an issue when investors gain supernormal profits due to skill, hard work, and just pure luck.

Fairness, however, does require all to have equal access to information. Thus, the availability of information is not due to lack of effort but lack of access. All information must be available for use in the market. How investors use and what they make of the information determines success in the markets. In today's financial markets, information is readily available if one is willing to spend time and effort obtaining and analyzing the information. There is no shortage of channels, from social media, to trade journals, analyst reports, and everything else that is online. However, insider information is not available on any of these channels, no matter how hard one works to obtain the information. Instead, the information is released only to particular individuals in their organizations. These individuals are those identified by the SEC as officers, directors, employees of corporations; their friends, business associates, family members; employees of companies who provide services to corporations that have insider information.[2] Why should these individuals be able to profit from information not available to everyone else? The fairness argument rests on the fact these individuals make supernormal profits by trading the inside information obtained from their positions and not from their own skill, experience, or effort. Thus, Lori Loughlin, the television celebrity, paying $500,00 to get her two daughters admitted into the University of Southern California as crew recruits even though neither girl participated in the sport, is particularly galling for the average fair-minded person, not born into privilege.[3] Worse yet, her daughter, Olivia Jade Loughlin, who has pretensions of fame as a YouTuber, was uncontrite and oblivious to the deprivations of the 99 percent.

Fiduciary Duty

Nearly everyone deemed an insider is likely to have a fiduciary duty to serve the interests of the corporation and its shareholders. If employees are allowed to legally trade on insider information, they may spend more effort on pursuing their own interests rather than the interests of shareholders and the corporation. The corporation itself may attempt to tailor its release of information for maximum benefit to insiders. More importantly, the opportunity to engage in insider trading may undermine the relation of trust essential for business organizations.

Courts in the U.S. agree with the judgment that insiders in corporations have a fiduciary duty to serve shareholders and are in breach of this duty if they trade on the information gained as a corporate insider. The U.S. Supreme Court in *U.S. v. O'Hagan* upheld the fiduciary duty argument for corporate insiders. O'Hagan was a partner in a Minneapolis law firm advising the British company, Grand Metropolitan, in a hostile takeover of the U.S. company, Pillsbury Company.[4] O'Hagan tricked a fellow partner into revealing details of the takeover and made a profit of US$4.3 million through trading Pillsbury stock and stock options.

The appellate court ruled that O'Hagan did not engage in insider trading because he had no fiduciary duty to Pillsbury. Although O'Hagan misappropriated confidential information from his law firm, he did not perpetrate a fraud against it or Grand Metropolitan. O'Hagan would have been guilty of insider trading only if he were an insider at Pillsbury.

The U.S. Supreme Court overturned this lower court ruling in a six-to-three decision. The highest court affirmed the misappropriation theory.

According to the decision, a person commits securities fraud when she "misappropriates confidential information for securities trading purposes, in breach of fiduciary duty owed to the source of the information." In other words, an insider does not need to be a person in a company or one who is directly providing services to the company whose stock is traded. Even a person not directly working with the company but is in an organization providing a service to either the bidder or the target of the tender offer is an insider. Therefore, people entrusted with information and who trade on this information are considered by the law to be misappropriating, or stealing, the information.

Utilitarian Assessment

The utilitarian evaluation weighs the positive consequences versus the negative consequences of insider trading. The consequences measured should cover a broad array of interests including societal benefits and costs.

Positive Outcomes

On the benefits side of a utilitarian analysis, some empirical research shows security prices will better and faster reflect fundamental value by incorporating private information due to the transactions of insiders. Faster and efficient price discovery improves the optimal allocation of scarce financial resources at a fair price. This is a central function of stock markets in an economy. For efficient information dissemination and price discovery, insider trading creates another channel for conveying information. Arguably, some market information is diffuse and complex, perhaps not easily conveyed in public announcements. Sometimes information pertaining to valuing an asset or revenue stream may not be channeled effectively. In such cases, insider trading may possibly act as an efficient replacement for public disclosure.[5]

The second benefit espoused by insider trading proponents is the increase in market liquidity that comes from the activity. The evidence on this issue is mixed as Kyle predicts less liquid stock markets while Grossman and Holden and Subrahmanyam predict markets will be more liquid.[6,7,8] Different results emerge from different assumptions about the relative importance of insiders, liquidity traders, noise traders, or market makers.

The third benefit of insider trading is the incentive it gives for corporate managers to take risks and therefore, possibly increase the shareholder value of the company. Not unlike other stock compensation schemes, if managers are allowed to trade on inside information, they are likely to engage in activities that will benefit the stock price of the company, such as increasing sales through innovative schemes or embarking on revenue-generating projects. Managers know the revenues generated by these projects before the information is public and make profits from the insider trading. Thus, the argument goes, insider trading by corporate executives results in enhancing shareholder value, but possibly at the expense of other stakeholders.

The above arguments are market efficiency arguments. They are not ethical arguments but economic ones. Economic arguments about market efficiency give almost exclusive weight to the positive outcomes of faster and better price discovery for traded securities, but little to the adverse consequences of legalized insider trading. What are the negative consequences of insider trading? These disbenefits arise from the belief the market is rigged. Investors may perceive the stock market as an unlevel playing field and be less inclined to participate. The lack of participation can lead to two poor outcomes: (1) a fall in the volumes traded in markets that lessen the efficiency of price discovery, and (2) a belief financial markets are structured for the privileged few, which leads to disillusionment with the financial and even perhaps, the economic system. This dissatisfaction, if it gets severe enough, may ultimately lead to social unrest, as we now occasionally witness in the U.S. In addition, investors may feel they have to adopt costly defensive measures. Eventually volumes will fall as will market liquidity. The market is left to the use of professional investors and high-frequency traders.

When those who claim insider trading is not unethical measure its benefits and costs, they surmise it is difficult to find damage done by insider trading.[9] They stress the informational gains, which lead to better prices guiding capital formation in the economy. Yet, the evidence that insider trading does not harm liquidity and volumes is inconclusive. This lack of evidence is mainly because insider trading is illegal, and it is difficult to set up a controlled situation to measure the effects of legalized insider trading. Crucially, proponents of insider trading argue for the benefits solely through the lens of modern finance theory, ignoring other models of analyzing markets, specifically behavioral models of finance.

Negative Outcomes: Applying Behavioral Economics to Insider Trading

The concept of trust is absent in modern finance theory and yet that virtue is of prime importance in business and financial relationships. Market efficiency proponents of insider trading seem assured that by improving the efficiency of the security market, the confidence of a rational investor in that market will not be damaged. That (mythical) rational investor finds it irrelevant if the insider trader earns abnormal profits. More important that market prices reflect every piece of information. Note the assumption of the "rational investor," an assumed entity who does not mind abnormal profits gained unfairly. The rational investor is rational in one sense only: her sole utility preference is profit maximization and her sole motivation is self-interest. As discussed in Chapter 2, this archetypal investor does not exist. The conclusion rational investors in the markets are unfazed by insider trading is unsound and unrealistic because the assumption all investors are rational, in the neo-liberal economic sense, is wrong.

Applying behavioral finance to insider trading gives us different conclusions from those using modern finance theory. Results of behavioral economic studies such as the ultimatum game, demonstrate people are not purely self-interested, but instead are motivated by the principle of fairness. Two players participate in the ultimatum game. Player 1 is the proposer and is given a large sum of money. Player 2 is the responder. The proposer offers a certain amount of her initial funds to the responder. The responder can either accept or reject the offer. If the responder rejects the offer, both players lose the initial sum of money. If the responder accepts the offer, both players keep their respective share of the money. If both players are "rational" agents, the proposer should offer to share a small percentage of the initial sum, perhaps 5 percent. A rational economic agent will accept the offer because the small amount is better than a zero amount. However, results of this experiment across cultures and time show this type of rational expectation behavior is largely absent. The typical allocation is 20–50 percent. Responders who are offered less than 20 percent generally refuse the offer. This behavior surely does not accord with the rational expectations model. Players are instead driven by the concept of fairness. Responders prefer to take nothing rather than accept an offer that seems to them unfair. Thus, the principle of fairness has intrinsic value to them, and they are prepared to uphold the principle even in the face of certain monetary loss.

Apply the result of the ultimatum game to insider trading and it's not a logical leap to infer investors will view gains made from such activity as unfair enrichment. Market participants not in the privileged position to gain from insider trading are then likely to reject the market and withdraw. Players will do so despite the arguments that insider trading increases the speed of price discovery, leading to more efficient pricing of securities and benefitting the market as a whole. As long as there are people not benefitting from insider trading and who view gains from insider trading as unfair, there is the strong likelihood these people will not participate in or may even disrupt the securities markets.

A striking example of disruption, perhaps the first of many to come, occurred in the U.S. stock markets in January 2021. Shares in a U.S. games company, GameStop, soared more than 700% in a week.[10] The video games retailer is a relic in a world moving online (the company made a loss of $795 million in 2019). Not surprisingly, major hedge funds bet against the stock by shorting it. Day traders, disparagingly classified as amateurs and retail investors by so-called market professionals, swapping tips on social media sites such as Reddit, and in coordinated moves, drove up the share price. The amateur investors say they are just playing Wall Street at its own game. As evidenced by a multitude of posts on r/WallStreetBets, investing in GameStop was a way to spread a message about the power of that community against a system rigged against them. The collective push by online investors sought to fight back against a system they feel deserved reckoning and to unleash general chaos. Contrary to the Friedmanite stance on markets, some of the day traders were willing to risk their money to make a point over an unjust financial reality. To quote one post on Reddit "I YOLO'd (you only live once) my life savings because I was never going to retire anyway."[11] Indeed this sort of behavior is contrary to the expectations of those who argue investors will not lose confidence in the market because they are "rational agents" interested only in profit maximization and driven by self-interest. In other words, from a behavioral finance standpoint, insider trading could result over time, especially in an era of rising inequality, in a severe loss of trust, lower liquidity in the market, and as we saw with GameStop, growing market disruption.

If we weigh the above outcome against the benefits of insider trading propounded by market efficiency advocates, a significant measure of doubt exists on whether the utilitarian calculation shows that good outcomes outweigh the bad ones. The ethics of insider trading should not be considered only using modern finance theory. Rather, behavioral finance theory should also be applied to the ethical analysis of insider trading.

RIGHT ACTION: DON'T BE SEDUCED BY THE MONEY

Do not succumb to the pressure to produce, through unethical means, above average returns or be seduced by the money. Quite simply, don't engage in insider trading.

To be honest, this prescription is hard to follow, and many do succumb. Several reasons account for this outcome. First, the amounts of money can be enormous. Suppose a hedge fund manages US$2 billion and charges a two-and-twenty rate. If the market return is 10 percent for the year and the fund returns 15 percent, the fund will earn 20 percent of the five percent above the market return. The above market return comes out to US$100 million. The performance fee is 20 percent of the US$100 million, which is US$20 million. If the fund returns 20 percent then the performance fee comes out to US$40 million. Thus, the greater the outperformance the more lucrative the performance fees. The temptation to cheat for this level of reward seduces people who in general started out as honest and law-abiding people. But in a good year, the US$40 million will mean bonuses amounting to millions of dollars.

The second reason for falling into the money seduction trap lies in the equation of money with success and ultimately with happiness. That equivalence is a societal peculiarity of our times. We may blame this particular condition on capitalism of the neo-liberal kind. Interestingly, in ancient Greece, money was not equated with success. Admiration was not heaped on merchants unlike our contemporary adulation of wealthy CEOs, IT entrepreneurs, private equity moguls, and hedge fund managers. Ancient Greeks admired heroes who gained social reverence from brave deeds in battle. Deeds that became legend and were woven into epic poems. Achilles in Homer's *Iliad* sought glory, won only on the battlefield. Glory or *kleios* in Greek, was the currency of greatness and success. Merchants with money were tolerated but not admired. Times change and we now have free market capitalism that extols wealth as greatness. Times will change again, invariably.

NOTES

1. "College Admissions Scandal," *The New York Times*, https://www.nytimes.com/news-event/college-admissions-scandal. Accessed June 8, 2020.
2. Kara Tan Bhala, Warren Yeh and Raj Bhala, *International Investment Management: Theory, Ethics and Practice* (London, UK: Routledge, 2016), 324.
3. Kate Taylor, "Lori Loughlin Pleads Guilty via Zoom in College Admissions Case," *The New York Times*, May 22, 2020, https://www.nytimes.com/2020/05/22/us/lori-loughlin-pleads-guilty.html. Accessed June 8, 2020.
4. Tan Bhala et al. (2016), 325.
5. P.J. Engelen and L.V. Liedekerke, "Insider Trading." *Finance Ethics: Crititcal Issues in Theory and Practice*, ed. John R. Boatright (Hoboken, NJ: John Wiley & Sons, Inc, 2010), 201.
6. A. Kyle, "Continuous Auctions and Insider Trading." *Econometrica*, Vol. 53, (1985), 1315–1336.
7. S. Grossman, "An Analysis of the Role of Insider Trading on Futures Markets." *Journal of Business*, Vol. 59 (1986), 129–146.
8. C. Holden and A. Subrahmanyam, "Long Lived Private Information and Imperfect Competition." *Journal of Finance*, Vol. 47 (1992), 247–270.
9. Engelen and Liedekerke (2010), 207.
10. BBC News. "Gamestop: 'Failing' Firm Soars in Value as Amateurs Buy Stock" (January 27, 2021) https://www.bbc.com/news/business-558 17918. Accessed January 28, 2021.
11. Time, "Revenge Tactic: GameStop's Massive Stock Surge Isn't Only About Making Money" (January 28, 2021) https://time.com/5933931/gamestop-stock-market-reddit-money/ Accessed January 28, 2021.

CHAPTER 7

Hedge Fund Harassment Case Study

The Story: Hedge Fund Boss Behaving Badly

For the rest of my short-lived time at the hedge fund, I studiously avoided the temptation to obtain insider information (see previous chapter). What made me eventually leave the company a year later was the hostile workplace environment. The harassment came from the top, from one person, the Owner.

I entered the hedge fund company as a part-time investment professional working three days a week. After six years out of the investing ecosystem, I thought much would have changed in this biome. But to my surprise and relief, I observed few changes. Data were still largely obtained via a Bloomberg terminal, equity analysts investigated companies in much the same way, portfolio managers used familiar allocation tools and strategies, and customers still needed to be sold the investment story. The big change for me was moving from a large Fortune 500 company, with professional standards and operating procedures (including workplace harassment complaint procedures), to a small owner-led company with fewer than 20 employees. Working on the fly is the phrase that comes

---

Supplementary Information The online version contains supplementary material available at https://doi.org/10.1007/978-3-031-34401-5_7.

to mind when I relive my time at that company. I had once worked in this same type of environment when I first started out with an undergraduate degree in Systems and Management. The experience was traumatic, but I might have suppressed memories of that slice of life because I did not have reservations about accepting yet another job offer from the owner and founder of a small business. Human selective memory is a wonder. This unconscious deletion of painful bits of memory causes us to leap into situations that may, on occasion perhaps, end up brilliantly because we took the risk. More likely, we repeat the same mistakes after failing to learn from the past. Over my time at the hedge fund, memories of my previous ill-fated job started coming back to me as unhappy but familiar situations presented themselves.

I recall my first day of work, when I joined the daily, all company meeting to discuss investment issues on portfolio companies. The Owner led discussions and called on staff for updates and answers to every type of question. Fair enough and pretty standard. As the meeting progressed, his voice would get louder and his speech would be increasingly laced with profanities. He would literally yell at staff members when they had not done as he expected, or the outcome of their work was below his expectations, dropping the "F" bomb with the frequency of simple articles of language. He would shout out commands like, "Call the (expletive) managing director and find out what's the (expletive) is happening!" or "What the (expletive) do I pay you for, you're not getting me anything useful!" I sat there dumbfounded as my new colleagues submissively accepted this verbal abuse. Apparently, it was just another day in the life of a battered employee at a hedge fund. My heart sank and anxiety seeped into my soul. What had I gotten myself into, I asked myself silently as I watched the unexpected horror show. When the Owner interviewed me for the job, he seemed to be intelligent, experienced, decent, but also a typical Wall Street tell-it-as-it-is type of man. He never raised his voice once during our conversations. I began to realize he was a Janus type personality. Charming and intelligent to some but bellicose and angry to subordinates. The Owner was an abusive supervisor. His abuse and mistreatment fell into three categories: verbal abuse (yelling and belittling subordinates), demanding staff perform tasks unrelated to their jobs, and generating a hostile work environment.

Verbal Abuse

Each day would see a dispiriting repeat of the morning yelling sessions. The man apparently reveled in office-centered yelling and publicly ridiculing staff. The workspace was his special place where he could show the other face of his Janus personality. When I recall the migraine inducing shouts, I am reminded of the 1994 George Huang movie *Swimming with Sharks*.

> What did I tell you the first day? Your thoughts are nothing; you are nothing…who do you think you are, you snot-faced little punk? Let me make this clear for you, OK, and now try to follow me, because I'm going to be moving in a kind of a circular motion, but if you pay attention, there will be a point. You are nothing. If you were in my toilet bowl I wouldn't bother flushing it. My bathmat means more to me than you…you don't like it here, leave!

These infamous words spew out of the mouth of Buddy Ackerman, a powerful movie producer and the boss from hell. Buddy is the quintessential abusive supervisor.[1] He was humiliating his assistant Guy, who stuck around for the abuse because he thought he needed the job to break into the movie business. Many of us think the same way, each stuck in her own workplace abuse nightmare, trying to accumulate experience, credibility, and money.

Over time, I noted the Owner would abuse some employees more than others. One member of the investment team, A, was a timid man who was on a work visa. His residency in the U.S. was tied to his job at the hedge fund. Lose the job, lose his U.S. residency. That was A's kryptonite and the Owner knew it. For this reason and because of his mild personality, A seemed to be the recipient of more shouts, expletives, and unreasonable demands. A would be frequently asked to carry out the Owner's and his wife's personal chores.

Tasks Unrelated to Work

One Sunday afternoon, as I sat in my dining room playing UNO, a mindless but addictive card game, with my daughter, I received a call from the Owner.

"Hey, can you go to the airport and pick up my wife? She's arriving this evening from California at 7:20 pm. Just drive to the airport, pick her up and drop her at our place," he said in a commanding tone.

I sat in confounded silence for a few seconds because last time I looked, my official designation at the company was portfolio manager, not chauffeur. The last time I looked, he and I were nowhere near, "friend driving friend's wife from airport," status.

I eventually said, "Um, sorry I'm busy right now and it'll take me an hour to drive to the airport and another 90 minutes to drop her off at your home and then drive back to my place." There was a pause at the end of the other line (time to get over the shock of rejection perhaps).

"Oh, it's just that I'm busy with work here," he said, sounding irritated. Uncomfortable silence.

"Sorry. Sunday's my time with family," I said.

"Well, OK. I'll ask A to pick her up. That's fine. Enjoy your Sunday with family," he said curtly and hung up.

The request left me annoyed and humiliated. I was just a body to do menial, personal tasks for the boss, never mind my credentials and experience. What professional would subject herself to this type of shoddy treatment? Later, with a hopeless shrug, A told me he had picked up the Owner's wife at the airport and dropped her home.

A Hostile Work Environment

Each day as I entered the office, I would find myself physically tensing up. It was as if I was entering a shark tank, with just one large angry, unpredictable shark preying on anxious small fish. If I sat at my desk sipping a cup of coffee and the Owner spotted, what seemed to him to be an aberrant behavior (no one sits and does nothing in his office), he would stride over, hover at my desk and ask what I was doing at that moment.

"Just taking a short coffee break." I would say.

"What projects are you working on?" he would ask curtly.

I would tell him all the to do items I had on my work list.

"You should also call X about this matter. Right now, I need the information." he would demand, because he needed to know I had work to do.

This sequence of events repeated each day whenever I or anyone took just a brief break because a quick respite was equated with slouching on the job. As a result, everyone pretended to be busy at the computer, analyzing information, reading, or just generally busy, whenever the Owner appeared. It mattered little that I had run a multi-billion dollar fund far larger than the assets under management at this particular hedge fund. Apparently, running a mutual fund was for lethargic losers. In contrast, managing a hedge fund needed drive, energy, brilliance, hard work, and insatiable hunger for money. I was repeatedly prodded with this inane lecture, whenever I was seen as slowing down or lazing off.

Mistakes at work are unavoidable. Unfortunately, the discovery of mistakes by the Owner invariably resulted in ugly explosions of temper. Phrases like, "What do I pay you for?", "You're working for me and I expect you to not make (expletive) mistakes," were the norm during deranged high-volume tirades against cowering staff, whose mistakes were publicly aired. The mistreatment was clearly done with the aim of eliciting high performance or to send the message that mistakes would not be tolerated.

Ethics Issue: Maltreatment of Employees

The ethical problem in this case study is the mistreatment of employees. Is this type of treatment acceptable and if it is not acceptable from an ethics perspective, why? The staff at the hedge fund viewed their treatment by the Owner as unavoidable. They wanted to work for a hedge fund and get remunerated lavishly for their work. In return, they believed they could be subjected to this type of mistreatment because it was standard in the hedge fund industry. The staff endured the abuse, suffered the stress, and carried on believing it was just "life in high finance." Unfortunately, this attitude is too common in the finance industry. The type of behavior exhibited by the Owner is well documented and comes under the heading of **power harassment**. Power harassment includes a range of behaviors from mild irritation and annoyances to serious abuses which can even involve forced activity beyond the boundaries of the job description, such as picking a boss's spouse up from the airport on a Sunday. Power harassment falls under the general category of workplace harassment, which is the offensive, belittling behavior directed at an individual worker or group of workers. Aggressive behaviors have become a significant source of work stress, as reported by employees. Under occupational health and safety laws around the world, workplace harassment and workplace bullying are identified as being core psychosocial hazards.

Researchers use several different labels to refer to destructive supervisor behaviors comprising angry outbursts, public ridiculing, taking credit for subordinates' success, and scapegoating subordinates. The labels include petty tyranny, supervisor aggression, and supervisor undermining, but most of the work conducted to date employs the term abusive supervision. Tepper defines abusive supervision as subordinates' perceptions of the extent to which supervisors engage in the sustained display of hostile verbal and nonverbal behaviors, excluding physical contact.[2] Bies identifies the following manifestations of abusive supervision: public criticism, loud and angry tantrums, rudeness, inconsiderate actions, and coercion.[3] All these behavioral traits were exhibited by the Owner in this case study.

Abusive supervision affects an estimated 13.6% of U.S. workers, despite these behaviors incurring substantial costs.[4] The victims of non-physical managerial hostility report diminished well-being and quality of work life that can spill over to their lives away from work.[5] The cost to U.S. corporations of abusive supervision (in terms of absenteeism, health care costs, and lost productivity) is estimated in a 2006 study at $23.8 billion annually.[6] This loss is likely to have swelled over the past 17 years. Similar to abuse directed toward intimate partners, the elderly, and children, abusive supervision can be characterized as sustained or enduring in the sense it continues until (1) the victim terminates the relationship (2) the abuser terminates the relationship, or (3) the abuser modifies his or her behavior.[7] Not unusually, employees like those described in this case study (in particular, A) stay in these abusive relationships. Several features of abusive supervision contribute to their enduring quality. First, on the victims' side, many may remain in the relationships because they feel powerless to take corrective action. Others are economically dependent on the abusers. Yet others fear the unknown associated with separation more than they fear the abuse. Notably, victims may remain in the situation because the perpetrators often intersperse abusive behavior with normal behavior, in effect intermittently reinforcing the victim's hope the abuse will end. Second, because abusers often fail to recognize or take responsibility for their abusive behavior (which was certainly true in this case study), few modify their behavior. In many cases, even clinical intervention, as in studies of child abuse, fails to recast such relationships as non-abusive.

Ethics Analysis: It's About Human Dignity

From a human dignity perspective, treating employees and subordinates in a wretched manner demeans them as people and constitutes a gross violation of their human dignity. According to Kant, people have dignity or intrinsic worth because they are rational agents. Rationality confers free agency to people who are capable of making their own decisions, setting their own goals, and guiding their conduct by reason. Thus, human beings are not merely one valuable thing among others. Humans do the valuing and moral goodness exists because of the ability of human beings as rational beings to act from a good will. From a theological (Judeo-Christian-Islamic) perspective, human beings are always already invested with human dignity because they were created thus by a providential God. The reader should note therefore, both secular and religious arguments exist to support the proposition that human beings possess human dignity. As people have intrinsic worth, we have a moral obligation to treat human beings well. This includes promoting their welfare, respecting their rights, avoiding harm to them, and treating them with respect. In other words, we should not be abusing other people, whether they are subordinates at work or family members close to us.

From the perspective of natural law (see Chapter 5 for a fuller exposition), the first principle of this moral theory is to cause no harm. Undoubtedly, employee abuse by supervisors causes harm to the employee. Studies show subordinates whose supervisors were more abusive reported higher turnover, less favorable attitudes toward job, life, and organization, greater conflict between work and family life, and greater psychological distress.[8] The effects for job satisfaction, life satisfaction, family-to-work conflict, depression, and emotional exhaustion were more pronounced for abused subordinates with less job mobility. The links between abusive supervision and the various indexes of psychological distress are also troubling because even the milder manifestations may engender significant social and financial costs to organizations.

These costs would comprise the bulk of the negative outcomes that emerge from abusive supervision. If we conduct a utilitarian evaluation, we therefore expect the negative consequences of abusive behavior to outweigh the positive consequences. Tepper lists a host of adverse effects on employees who are targets of abusive supervision[9]:

1. Job dissatisfaction—likely results in subordinates seeking out and obtaining alternative employment.
2. Life dissatisfaction—bad work experiences translate into dissatisfaction with life.
3. Lack of commitment to the organization—commitment is not based on values or emotions but on economic need.
4. Psychological Distress—employees are likely to suffer depression, anxiety, loss of self-esteem, and emotional exhaustion.

There are also negative impacts on the organization from abusive supervision:

1. High turnover of staff—people ultimately leave their jobs. Three out of four victims and witnesses to bullying simply quit or are driven out. The loss of qualified personnel is a big financial cost because of the extensive hiring and training process for new workers.
2. Reduced productivity—targets of abuse tend to take more sick days. This cost tends to have a domino effect because other workers, non-targets, may be drawn into the fray and suffer personal stress that has a negative impact on their productivity as well.

The only positive outcome from abusive supervision I can think of is the temporary emotional high a supervisor may get from being abusive, and the satisfaction of a perverse psychological need arising from emotional deficiency.

By whatever standards of moral measure, abusive supervision is unethical. While few would dispute this conclusion, many in these sorts of situations, would simply shrug and continue to take the abuse. Workers, particularly in finance, do not see a way to get out of this type of situation without leaving the job and therefore, the money, behind. In a way, workers in finance, feel this type of "boot camp" is typical and expected in the industry. Finance departments of business schools further fuel this expectation when faculty and alumni relate tales of poor treatment of new recruits at investment banks, hedge funds, and private equity groups to naïve young MBA or BBA students. These "mentors" usually tell the stories with no ethics evaluation or discussion of values. Underlying their narratives is the unstated belief summed up by "you have to be tough in finance to succeed, otherwise, don't even go there." By not criticizing and objecting to abusive supervision, these teachers and role models implicitly condone the practice.

Right Action: Your Money or Your Life

Individuals

The assumption that abusive supervision is pervasive in the financial services industry is not wrong. The behavior is prevalent and the main form of workplace bullying in the U.S. The harms associated with abusive supervision are many, accruing to individuals and organizations. How much abuse a person will tolerate depends on the organizational and societal culture in which the behavior takes place.

Power distance describes the way people with varying degrees of power relate to one another, that is, the relationship between people with unequal status. The PDI, or power distance index, was developed through the answers to three key questions pertaining to frequency of (1) employees' being afraid to express disagreement with management, (2) subordinates' perception of their boss's actual decision-making process, and (3) subordinates' preference for their boss's style. Hofstede conducted his studies in 50 countries and 3 general regions. When reverse-ranked by PDI (lower scores indicating higher power distance acceptance), Norway and Sweden tie at 47/48, followed by Finland at 46, Great Britain at 44, Australia at 41, and the U.S. at only 38. The larger the power distance (and the lower the PDI ranking), the more likely hierarchy is accepted, subordinates expect to be told what to do, privileges for managers are the norm, inequalities are expected and tolerated, and values are authoritarian.[10] In addition, larger power distance signals an acceptance of the philosophy, "might makes right," that power is based on the ability to use force, autocracy is the managerial model, and the importance of the role of the manager is paramount. The PDI ranking suggests that workers in the U.S. are more comfortable with autocratic bosses than workers in the other countries listed and, possibly, more willing to accept their instructions. In the U.S. more abuse is done by managers, than by peers. We surmise from these data that workers in the U.S. tend to not join together to insist on workplace dignity. In addition, courts expect employees to have relatively thick skins. Behavior that is crude or obnoxious isn't usually grounds for a harassment lawsuit unless it targets people based on a protected characteristic (sex, age, race, disability, etc.). The "equal opportunity harasser" argument is apparently a good one to hang a boss's defense on. Yet, the literature on abusive bosses recommends staff talk to their peers about the problem. Some organizations select and train peer listeners to serve as compassionate experts, who advise their co-workers on bullying and harassment. Talking to peers and sharing frustrations may lessen the desire to leave an organization because, well, everyone is in the same position and each supports the other.

In terms of the hedge fund in this case study, turnover was abnormally high, which is in line with data from abusive supervisor studies. The abused staff did not stay in the company for long. The average time a staff member would stay on the job was roughly one to two years. The exception was A, who stayed with the hedge fund for close to ten years. In situations of this sort, the moment you feel the abuse is unbearable, begin the process of seeking a new job. While in that process, which may take more time than you would like, continue to talk to colleagues and those empathetic to your situation. Also, stand up to the abusive boss when he acts up. You don't have to raise your voice. Just say no, firmly, to ridiculous demands. Maintain your dignity by responding to shouts and profanities with simple statements like, "I heard you, there is no need to shout or curse." Speak up for your values and protect your human dignity. By doing so, you may even become a model of courage to others in your group who also are experiencing supervisory abuse. One of the best defense strategies is to do excellent, invaluable work so the boss has a strong motive not to upset you so much that you resign. Unless your supervisor is a complete psychopath (in which case, leave. Now), he will have his own self-interest in mind and attempt to be as pleasant as able, to keep you working for him.

Organizations

The role of the organization in deterring (vs. condoning) abuse cannot be overstated. Research is consistent with the idea that organizational norms, i.e., culture, play a powerful role in the occurrence of aggressive organizational behavior.[11] People behave more aggressively presumably because when others in their reference groups perform aggressive behaviors, employees view aggressive behavior as normal and acceptable. Hence, supervisors may be more likely to abuse their subordinates when they perceive such behavior to be a legitimate means of exercising authority in organizations. Any organization that truly wishes to discourage supervisor abuse or bullying needs a policy explicitly stating that this type of behavior will not be tolerated. An anti-abusive or bullying policy is a necessary condition for resolving complaints. Without such a policy, it is not possible to intervene on behalf of victims. Beyond a policy statement, an organization should have a code of conduct that provides concrete examples of desirable and forbidden behaviors. Just the process of developing the code of conduct helps raise awareness of inappropriate interactions.[12]

Of course, written documents are only effective if employees know about them and believe upper management stands behind them. Internal human resources professionals should be trained to promote a harassment-free workplace. New employees need training in how to treat others in the company and education on the organization's anti-harassment policy, where to report harassment and abuse, and procedures on tackling this type of behavior. Employees need to know where to turn if they are targets of abuse, or what consequences they will face if they abuse others.

When a complaint is lodged against a supervisor, standard operating procedures should kick in. Usually a grievance committee weighs the information provided by the victim, the accused, and any witnesses to determine the merits of the complaint. When formal interventions are used, more substantial training and rehabilitation are typically required to alter inveterate patterns of inappropriate behavior. If the harassment continues, the supervisor should be transferred to a position providing less opportunity to abuse (e.g. a non-supervisory capacity), or even terminated. By no means does this ideally just outcome happen in many instances. Hubert notes when a supervisor is valuable to the organization, anti-abuse protocol may fall by the way side as the target becomes a scapegoat: "The offender remains in the organization, the victim leaves, sometimes due to illness, sometimes through dismissal."[13] This unconscionable treatment of a victim is, regrettably, the norm when it comes to whistleblowers, as we shall see in the next chapter.

Notes

1. George Huang and Michael Lesslie. *Swimming with Sharks* (London, UK: Bloomsbury, 2014), 32.
2. Bennett J. Tepper. "Consequences of Abusive Supervision." *Academy of Management Journal*, Vol. 43, Issue 2 (April 2000), 178–190.
3. R.J. Bies and M.T. Tripp. "Two Faces of the Powerless: Coping with Tyranny." In R.M. Karamer and M.A. Neale (Eds.), *Power and Influence in Organizations* (Thousand Oaks, CA: Sage, 1996), 246–260.
4. A. Schat, S. Desmarais, and E. Kelloway. "Prevalence of Workplace Aggression in the U.S. Workforce: Findings from a National Study." In E.K. Kelloway, J. Barling, and J.J. Hurrell (Eds.), *Handbook of Workplace Violence* (Sage, CA: Thousand Oaks, 2006), 47–89.
5. Schat et al. (1996), 54–60.
6. B.J. Tepper, M.K. Duffy, C.A. Henle and L.S. Lambert. "Procedural Injustice, Victim Precipitation, and Abusive Supervision." *Personnel Psychology*, Vol. 59 (2006), 101–123.
7. Tepper (2000), 178.
8. Tepper (2000), 186.
9. Tepper (2000), 180–182.
10. Gina Vega and Debra R. Comer. "Sticks and Stones May Break Your Bones, But Words Can Break Your Spirit: Bullying in the Workplace." *Journal of Business Ethics*, Vol. 58 (2005), 101–109.
11. Bennett J. Tepper. "Abusive Supervision in Work Organizations: Review, Synthesis, and Research Agenda." *Journal of Management*, Vol. 33, Issue 3 (June 2007), 261–289.
12. Vega (2005), 107.
13. A.B. Hubert. "To Prevent and Overcome Undesirable Interaction: A Systematic Approach Model." In S. Einarsen, H. Hoel, D. Zapf, and C.L. Cooper (Eds.), *Bullying and Emotional Abuse in the Workplace: International Perspectives in Research and Practice* (London, UK: Taylor & Francis, 2003), 299–311.

CHAPTER 8

Whistleblowing Consultant Case Study

The Story: Whistleblowing or No Good Deed Goes Unpunished

Luck seemed to not favor me when I returned to the investment industry after an eight-year hiatus. I'm not sure how many women begin to doubt their abilities upon returning to paid work after taking an extended time off for family reasons. I know I did. Perhaps I lost my finance toughness. Could I still handle the rough and tumble of the macho male investment arena? Had I become a mom mimsy? These questions bothered me occasionally, especially in the midst of yet another stress inducing, bellowing session at the hedge fund (see previous chapter). The only way to remedy these self-doubts, I surmised, was to test myself in another investment management position.

After I quit the hedge fund, I plunged almost immediately into male-populated finance territory once again. I took on the position of consultant at a small mutual fund company (SMFC) run, once again, by a domineering male founder. To my defense, I did not know this extra

Supplementary Information The online version contains supplementary material available at https://doi.org/10.1007/978-3-031-34401-5_8.

and pretty key piece of information at the time of accepting the assignment. Yes, I know. I should have done my homework. In any case, I chalk this experience to destiny and the universe offering a learning experience. I thought, what dangers could there be for a paid consultant who was not an employee? Working part-time affords little chance of being embroiled in dire office politics. As a consultant, I carried out equity research on Asian stocks and made recommendations based on this research.

I worked for the most part, with two portfolio managers in the SMFC, both of whom were responsible for the international portions of equity portfolios. He was experienced and steady, she was fresh out of an Ivy League graduate business school and enthusiastic. We seemed to get along as a small internationally focused team and did I mention I was merely a consultant who did not want to get sucked into office politics? I simply went into the workplace one day a week and worked the rest of the time as needed, from home. The company was fine with me working from home (WFH) before this practice was forced on the world by a relentless coronavirus. This work arrangement may, at first glance, seem progressive. On the contrary, in dismal reality SMFC was stocked almost entirely with men in the investment department and was old school in structure. The founder had an authoritarian disposition, straddled late middle age, and was immersed in white privilege. The firm had around 15 portfolio managers. All save one were male (the recent graduate I worked with being the exception), and all were white. The company website page showing its portfolio management staff resembled a 1960s white manel (male panel). This company was not host to a hostile work environment as the previous hedge fund I worked at was, but neither did it have a culture that welcomed or actively supported diversity.

Nor was the SMFC oriented toward international investments. The firm offered one modest international equity fund to its investors. The management of the fund was sub-contracted out to another fund management company that purportedly had more international investing expertise. This type of arrangement is not unusual and is often done for cost-effectiveness reasons. The sub-manager did the actual portfolio management of the international fund. Our three-person team was tasked with making sure the equities in that portfolio were not duds. We did equity analysis, met with company management, and spoke regularly to sell side analysts about every stock in the international equity fund. It so happened the sub-manager ran and offered its own Asian equity fund. Unsurprisingly, the Asian stocks in SMFC's international fund matched closely with the stocks in the sub-manager's Asian equity fund. This too is not an issue. The problem arises, when the sub-manager front runs its client's mutual fund.

Front running is the practice of trading ahead of the trade of another investor. Usually this occurs when a broker gets an order from an institutional customer, such as a pension fund or mutual fund. Front running is an illegal practice. It also is unethical because this conduct unfairly uses information from the trade itself. In this case, the front running is done by the sub-manager. Say the sub-manager places an order to buy stock X for its own Asian equity fund at time T. Later, the sub-manager places an order to buy stock X for SMFC's international equity fund at time $T + 1$. If the stock is a small-cap stock with low liquidity, even a small buy order will push the price of X up to the benefit of the sub-manager's Asian equity portfolio. This practice is most advantageous at the end of the quarter when mandated quarterly reports must be publicly disclosed. Shareholders get an idea, albeit a little dated, about the state of a mutual fund at the close of quarter. Pushing up prices at this moment, increases the net asset value of a fund and improves the look of its performance.

After several months of consulting for SMFC, one of the members of the international team noticed trades of the same stocks were placed by the sub-manager for its Asian equity fund before trades were placed for the international equity fund of SMFC. He suspected the sub-manager of front-running SMFC's international equity fund. There was no definitive proof and we wondered if the timing was deliberate or just inadvertent due to a lack of manpower at the sub-manager and a chaotic management system. The member of the international team discussed his suspicions with me and suggested I write a memo to SMFC's CEO and founder of the firm detailing my suspicions and suggesting further investigations. I agreed with his assessment of the situation and was incensed the sub-manager could apparently perpetrate this act. As a consultant, I thought I had the moral obligation to point out problems in the system to my client and a fiduciary duty to put the interests of my client first. I had no idea this member of the international team was actually setting me up for failure. He was threatened by my presence, fearing I would soon want to be employed full time, and therefore, perhaps pushing ahead of him in promotion to senior portfolio manager of the international equity fund.

I wrote a well-worded, dispassionate, explanatory memo giving details of the possible front-running trades and advised, based on this evidence, the SMFC proceed with further investigation on this matter. Two hours after I handed the memo to the CEO's personal assistant, I was called into his office. From his red face and wide glassy eyes, I guessed he was livid; less because of the possible front running that occurred but because I had put my suspicions of the act on paper and was whistleblowing possible wrongdoing. He stood up from his chair behind his hefty mahogany desk and walked toward me in an attempt perhaps, to intimidate me. (Note to those with a diminutive stature, intimidation using the "towering over victim" method is hard to pull off.). He stood in front of my chair and began his interrogation, demanding to know why I wrote the memo and who I had spoken to about the issue.

"What kind of documentation do you have to support your case?" he asked. I noticed some perspiration on his upper lip. "Give me everything you have and all copies as well," he growled, overcompensating for his uneasiness, narrowing his eyes, ready for any protestation or further questioning on my part.

"OK, I'll get the papers together," I said, wanting to get out of this situation. Thinking the conversation was over, and uncomfortable with his close proximity to me, I got up to leave, taking a few steps back from him. As I turned to exit, he quickly started a spiel about how he hoped my working part-time in the office as a consultant would provide added resources to the international team, but my position was not working out as he had planned. (Definitely a bad prelude to a boss's evaluation of your work.) We eyed each other during the brief moment of silence. Then he fired me.

Alas, I had just suffered the usual sad end in the common tale of the ill-fated whistleblower.

Ethics Issue: Whistleblowing

There are two ethics issues in this case. The first is front running. This practice is obviously illegal and unethical. When brokers front run a client, the act hurts the customer if the front-running trade adversely changes the price the customer trades at, say, a buy order executed at a higher price or a sell order at a lower one. The broker is also hurting the party on the other side of the trade. The broker has an unfair information advantage about an impending change in price likely to occur when she places her customer's trade. In fact, the only way to make a profit from the trade is through information advantage. There is no talent involved in front running.

The second ethics issue is whistleblowing on which we focus for the rest of this analysis. Whistleblowing covers a wide range of activities that may be dissimilar from an ethics point of view. We encounter two generalizable forms of whistleblowing: internal and external.[1] Internal whistleblowing refers to disclosures by employees to executives within a firm, perhaps concerning improper conduct of fellow employees or bosses who are cheating or stealing from the company. In these cases, whistleblowing is the reporting of improper activities to an appropriate person. The disclosure of inappropriate conduct is made to someone within the organization or system. Generally, one believes an investigation will follow and a sanction imposed. In my case, I absolutely expected an investigation to follow my report of possible misconduct. Perhaps whistleblowers are idealists at heart believing people, especially those in authority, to be virtuous and guided by good conscience.

The other type of whistleblower does not enjoy any fairer outcomes. External whistleblowing occurs when the whistleblower makes public information the improper conduct of an employee or employees in an organization or serious defects in products manufactured by a company. Internal whistleblowing causes problems for the firm, which are for the most part restricted to those within the firm. External whistleblowing is of concern to the general public, because the public rather than the firm is threatened with harm. To further refine the categorization of whistleblowing, there is private sector and governmental whistleblowing. The former involves employees of private sector firms disclosing bad conduct or defective products. The latter refers to government employees who divulge to a governmental regulatory or investigative bureau unethical practice in their division or office and/or to employees within a firm that has government contracts who report fraud against the government. Sometimes whistleblowing refers to leaks by government employees to the media. Finally, there's the differentiation between personal whistleblowing, where the injured party of some misconduct is the whistleblower, and impersonal whistleblowing, where the potential or actual injury is to others or to the organization rather than to oneself. This case study falls into the category of impersonal, internal and external (see below), private sector whistleblowing.

ETHICS ANALYSIS: TO WHISTLEBLOW OR NOT, THAT IS THE QUESTION

Whichever the type of whistleblowing, companies invariably treat whistle-blowers poorly. Most, like me, are fired. In some instances, they are blackballed in the whole industry. If they are not fired, they are shunned and conveniently forgotten at promotion time. Only rarely have companies praised and promoted such people. The reason for this scandalous treatment is obvious. The whistleblower forces the company to do what it does not want to do, even if morally, it is the right action. There is ample evidence that when someone does blow the whistle on her company, even with ethical reasons, and with positive results for the public, she is generally ostracized, not only by management but also by fellow employees. These employees use the loyalty argument to justify their contempt of the whistleblower.

The argument goes something like this. When people join a company, they become part of an organization composed of fellow employees. I theorize people prefer to think, maybe consciously, but more likely in this cynical age of work, unconsciously, of their occupational places and their fellow sloggers as engaging in a noble quest, bound in fellowship. I attribute this belief to our primal collective unconscious, captured in epics like the *Lord of the Rings*, and during the U.S. presidential elections of 2020 (Sauron is the other party's presidential candidate, his followers are orcs, ours are elves from Lothlorien no less, or humans from Gondor naturally, etc.). The nerd lights are flashing red so back to point, when it comes to companies and employees, people aren't robots but have feelings and are part of a joint enterprise. In accepting employment, employees at every level owe something to the employing firm and to those with whom they work. Thus, the anti-whistleblower argument asserts employees owe not only a certain amount of work but also a certain positive attitude toward that work and to their fellow workers. Without, let's call it loyalty, a worker is either indifferent or disaffected. An indifferent or disaffected worker is clearly not a team player and typically contributes only enough work to keep her from being fired. Given the chance, such a worker would gladly leave the firm for a job with another company. Such employees lack loyalty to their company. If the disaffected worker were to blow the whistle on her employer, others in the company will doubt she did so from noble or moral motives (Didn't Boromir try to steal the ring from Frodo in a power grab thus endangering the fellowship!?). Such doubts may be misplaced, but the natural tendency is to see whistleblowing as stemming from the worker's indifference or disaffection. Hence, it is unlikely those workers who feel a sense of obligation or loyalty to the firm will look kindly on the whistleblower or on whistleblowing. Indeed, it was so with my fellow workers at SMFC. None said anything to me when I left. The two people with whom I worked closely on the international team did not approach me or discuss the memo with me, even though I had written the piece with their full knowledge. One had even read the memo and made some edits. They remained loyal to SMFC and their co-workers, dismissing me apparently without much thought. Such a dispiriting outcome explains why whistleblowers are uncommon and companies get away with a lot of bad practices and unethical behavior.

Even if we concede an employee should feel some loyalty to a firm and her fellow workers, we cannot agree such loyalty involves or demands a worker engage in immoral activities for the firm. Loyalty does not necessarily override other moral considerations in whistleblowing. Those who claim whistleblowing is always immoral to make loyalty to a firm the worker's highest obligation and consider it to be always overriding.[2] They do not consider the possibility an employee might blow the whistle out of loyalty to the firm, if the employee believes that those engaged in certain behaviors are harming the company.

Was I doing the ethically right act when I reported to the CEO my suspicions of front running by the sub-manager of the fund? Three criteria measure whether a whistleblowing act is morally permissible and two additional criteria determine if it is morally *required*. These standards apply to external whistleblowing where the whistle is blown outside the company and where harm is thought to be inflicted on the public by a defective product or service. Front running of a fund would harm both the fund company and members of the public who own shares in the fund. The company would suffer legal consequences, if regulators take a hard stance on the offense, as well as severe reputational damage. Public shareholders of the fund are harmed because they will not receive fair pricing on their shares if they sell or buy them during the time when the front running occurred. Instead the price would have been manipulated. In this case study therefore, harm is threatened to both the company and the public, making it an internal and external type of whistleblowing.

The business ethicist, Richard De George, gives a checklist to determine if whistleblowing is morally permissible[3]:

1. The firm, through its practices, will do serious and considerable harm to employees or to the public, i.e., the user of the product or service, an innocent bystander, or the general public.
2. Once employees identify a serious threat to the user of the product or service or to the public, they should report the problem to their immediate superior and make their moral concern known. Crucially, this step gives the company first chance to correct the misconduct.
3. If one's immediate supervisor does nothing effective about the concern or complaint, the employee should exhaust the internal procedures and possibilities within the firm. Take the matter up to the highest level if necessary.

According to this checklist, my whistleblowing was clearly morally permissible. My colleague on the international team first alerted me to the front-running possibility. Indeed, he gave me much of the evidence I subsequently gave to the CEO.[4] I decided the harm done to the company and to our shareholders merited my taking the problem to the highest level. In addition, as a consultant, I owed the company a duty to protect its interests and reputation.

Most times, after a whistleblower informs the upper levels of management about the misconduct in a company, she is then summarily dismissed from employment. My experience was therefore, no different from the typical whistleblower's. Following her dismissal, the whistleblower is morally obliged to then go public with the information if the following criteria are met:

4. The whistleblower must have, or have accessible, documented evidence that would convince a reasonable, impartial observer of the whistleblower's assessment of the situation. The company's product or service must pose a serious and likely danger to the public.
5. The employee must have good reasons to believe that by going public the necessary changes will be brought about. The chance of being successful must be worth the risk in endangering the whistleblower.

Depending on an individual's view of the moral importance of whistleblowing, conditions (4) and (5) above may be either too lax or too stringent. Those who think big corporations almost always take the unethical road when not under close scrutiny will see these standards as too stringent. Harm to the public is a serious matter and the potential whistleblower should be heroic and willing to sacrifice her job and her future career success to prevent harm to others. Such tough standards will give whistleblowers an out from their duty to protect the public.

Those who think (4) and (5) are overly lax, argue that making whistleblowing a moral obligation too readily will encourage whistleblowing willy-nilly, thereby reducing the effectiveness of the act. This group of people think whistleblowing is a supererogatory act. This fearsome phrase simply signifies an act that goes beyond our moral obligation or duty. Supererogatory acts are morally good but not strictly required. In the case of whistleblowing, although we are not permitted to act immorally, we have no general moral obligation to prevent all others from acting immorally. To rebut this argument, we can say whistleblowing is an act in which one attempts to prevent harm to a third party. It is not implausible to claim both that we are morally obliged to prevent harm to others at relatively little expense to ourselves, and we are morally obliged to prevent great harm to a great many others, even at considerable harm to ourselves.

Right Action: Consider Options Rationally, Then If You Can or Must, Whistleblow

The five conditions in the previous section are a useful guide for those who need help deciding whether whistleblowing in their situation is morally permissible (you *can* blow the whistle) or morally required (you *must* blow the whistle). The point is to not seek automatic rules but to learn to consider and weigh the pertinent factors in each case. As with every case study in this book, I urge you to discuss the problem with close relatives and friends you trust. You need not decide alone in a sad vacuum.

Should I have blown the whistle to management in this case study? If we consider this incident as an instance of internal, non-personal whistleblowing, there appears to be a clear threat of harm to the company. The sub-manager of the SMFC fund was likely acting against the welfare of the firm and it could not claim a right to privacy with respect to its actions, and no immunity from being reported. The CEO of SMFC certainly had the right and the obligation to stop the misconduct. Hence, I was ethically correct to stop that activity. This case also is an instance where harm is not only caused to the firm but also to the public. Scholars and practitioners offer little argument that shareholders and potential shareholders of the fund are harmed by price manipulation caused by front running. Therefore, condition (1) above is met and I was morally permitted to blow the whistle to my superiors.

Should I have blown the whistle to the public after I was canned? I do not believe conditions (4) and especially (5) were met. There would be harm done to shareholders, but the harm would not have been to their physical well-being and was not in the least, life threatening. In addition, I believed the CEO would take the necessary actions after he learned of the possible misconduct. And indeed, he eventually did. He dismissed the sub-manager and gave the responsibility of managing the international fund to his internal team.[5] If I had gone public with my information, I would have encountered a legal suit from the SMFC that would have required inordinate amounts of time and treasure to fend off. In addition, there could have been much unwanted publicity and consequently, damage to my reputation and ability to find future work. I was not prepared to endanger my family and myself with these unpalatable outcomes. Unfortunately, these are the realities of whistleblowing.

Federal and state whistleblower protection laws exist to protect both public and private employees who are fired for reporting violations of the law and/or misconduct against their employers. For instance, federal whistleblower protection laws, such as key environmental laws including the federal Clean Air Act, Toxic Substance Control Act, The Pollution Prevention Act and other OSHA Whistleblower Protections make it unlawful to fire employees in retaliation for filing a claim or reporting violations, including health and safety hazards, and financial misappropriation. In addition to federal whistleblower protection laws, most U.S. states make it unlawful to fire employees for reporting employer violations and other acts of misconduct. However, a company that wishes to be moral, i.e., not engage in harmful practices or produce harmful products, can take steps to preclude the necessity of whistleblowing. Indeed, if a company wishes to foster both collegiality and honesty among its employees, then it should implement and actively practice policies that help employees work through their responsibilities with respect to issues involving ethical breaches by superiors and colleagues.

NOTES

1. Richard T. De George, *Business Ethics (6th Edition)* (Upper Saddle River, NJ: Pearson Prentice Hall, 2006), 300.
2. De George (2006), 306.
3. De George (2006), 308–313.
4. Yes, I know, I was set up. This colleague was probably threatened by my presence and I represented to him a possible rival to his ascension up the greasy pole. He hoped I would blow the whistle, betting his CEO, whom he had worked with for years, would react by terminating my position.
5. Thus, my male colleague in the international succeeded, perhaps well beyond his expectations. He was given responsibility of the fund.

CHAPTER 9

Finance Academy Gender Inequity Case Study

THE STORY: GENDER DISCRIMINATION IN THE FINANCE ACADEMY

The last stop on my finance career highway was the political minefields of academia. This destination was an unexpected, mostly unenjoyable, endpoint to my stimulating and lucrative journey in financial services. Still, bad experiences offer lessons, especially in ethics. I had not given much thought to entering the academy, as my ultimate goal was to start the first and (still) world's only independent think tank dedicated to the promotion, research, and education in financial ethics. (I liked this line so much that it became my eventual elevator pitch). The concept was in place and I planned on becoming a social entrepreneur, building from ground up, a new intellectual enterprise. But the finance gods were not quite done with me.

After several social encounters, an acquaintance I had first met at one of my public lectures invited me to join the finance department in the business school of a public university. Accordingly, let's call that business school of a public university its acronym, BSPU. This person was a

---

Supplementary Information The online version contains supplementary material available at https://doi.org/10.1007/978-3-031-34401-5_9.

K. Tan Bhala, *Ethics in Finance*,
https://doi.org/10.1007/978-3-031-34401-5_9

lecturer in the finance department and well respected at BSPU. Upon first glance she seemed to have more than a moderate amount of influence in the department. After a couple of rounds of interviews with the Associate Dean and the Dean, I was offered an adjunct position to lecture on the topic of work and institutions in financial services. The position seemed to have synergies with my plans, and teaching at BSPU seemed a logical segue into think tank development. I was to teach on a part-time basis, offering a two-hour class once a week. There was little interaction with other faculty members, as many were ensconced in their silos, emerging for faculty meetings and political skirmishes. In this simple assignment, working a few hours a week, in the ivory tower, away from corporate greed, not much could possibly go wrong, I thought naively.

The idealized image of the life of a college professor is just that: idealized. This version of the profession pictures a truth-seeking person, imbued with intellectual honesty, earnest in her pursuit of ideas, open to new viewpoints, and motivated to teach truth to young minds. Yet, the celebrated aphorism routinely attributed to Henry Kissinger "Academic politics are so vicious precisely because the stakes are so small," in my experience with the finance academy, is pretty accurate. In his speech for the John M. Ashbrook Memorial Dinner at Ashland University, Kissinger goes on to say, "I formulated the rule that the intensity of academic politics and the bitterness of it is in inverse proportion to the importance of the subject they're discussing. And I promise you at Harvard, they are passionately intense and the subjects are extremely unimportant."[1] I was not expecting to be in a rarefied atmosphere of pure intellectual pursuit, but was still somewhat surprised by the reality of the BSPU academic setting. Nassim Nicholas Taleb spent most of his life trading and investing in markets, i.e., in the practice of finance. And then, like me (except for his far greater wealth and fame), he spent some time in the finance academy, i.e., in the teaching of finance. From his brief immersion in the academy, he concludes:

> But academics (particularly in social science) seem to distrust each other; they live in petty obsessions, envy, and icy-cold hatreds, with small snubs developing into grudges, fossilized over time in the loneliness of the transaction with a computer screen and the immutability of their environment. Not to mention a level of envy I have almost never seen in business.... My experience is that money and transactions purify relations; ideas and abstract matters like "recognition" and "credit" warp them, creating an

atmosphere of perpetual rivalry. I grew to find people greedy for credentials nauseating, repulsive, and untrustworthy.[2]

I figure Taleb had some nasty run-ins with his colleagues in the academy.

Academics prize their "collegiality" and "intellectual autonomy." The former is largely mythical and university professors will engage in furious fights over the latter, especially if they believe they are ceding prized territory. I therefore encountered vicious resistance when I proposed teaching a new course on financial ethics to undergraduate business majors. In my mind, the course would benefit students who, I found after a few years of conversations in the classroom, lacked ethical decision-making tools. I believed teaching students frameworks for ethical analysis would help them navigate the financial services industry with integrity, honesty, and a level of unconflicted confidence. At least we could attempt to instill some notion of the worthiness of ethics.

I had started teaching this course to MBAs in a satellite location a few semesters after I was invited to lecture at BSPU. The offsite classrooms were distant from the main campus of BSPU. This satellite campus provided, for the most part, classes for students who were employed fulltime and doing a part-time MBA. The financial ethics class was low key, with a small enrolment. In other words, it was unthreatening to faculty members. Besides, the MBA program at BSPU was unranked and considered a poor stepchild of the school. The high status, money generating program for BSPU was the bachelor's in business administration (BBA), a popular undergraduate business major. It so happened curriculum change was taking place in the undergraduate business programs. A faculty committee had, naturally, been set up to design a new, improved curriculum. My enthusiastic response was to send a proposal for a course in financial ethics for undergraduates in business who chose to specialize in finance. To my astonishment, not only did the finance faculty reject my proposal, they also canceled my financial ethics class for MBAs. It was crystal clear they did not want me to teach ethics to students in finance.

Now a little more information about the composition of the finance faculty at BSPU. There was not a single woman who was tenured or on tenure track in the finance department of BSPU. Zero. Out of approximately 25 faculty members in the finance department, no woman possessed tenure or was hired with the expectation of being considered for tenure. Two women, including the one who invited me to join the faculty, were lecturers. There were a couple of men of color. The majority of the faculty were white men. Looking back at the demographics of the finance department, I should have figured out sooner that problems would arise.

Feeling dismissed without reason or discussion, I asked for a meeting of the full faculty so I could put my case forward for continuing to teach financial ethics to MBAs and starting a financial ethics course to undergraduates. Note to reader: the world had just suffered through the 2008 Global Financial Crisis, a catastrophic event triggered by greed, regulatory capture, excessive compensation, and a whole lot of bad ethics in financial services. Would not a course in financial ethics to finance undergraduates therefore, be an absolute godsend? Finance faculty at BSPU didn't think so.

The Meeting

In preparing for this meeting, I drew on decades of experience arguing for and marketing my products or ideas to others, many of whom were men. For example, I sold top management at the mutual fund company in which I worked, on the concept of offering an emerging markets fund. This development was a multimillion-dollar undertaking, involving multiple departments. I was put in charge of the endeavor after the president and chief financial officer both agreed to setting my idea into operation. Surely then, it was not a leap to think I could do a decent job persuading 25 academics on the worthiness of offering a financial ethics course after the worst financial crisis since the 1929 stock market crash which presaged the Great Depression. I was wrong!

First, I underestimated the veracity of Kissinger's statement about small matters with low stakes taking on tremendous significance in academic politics. Second, I underestimated the degree of implicit bias male faculty in the finance academy harbor against women. Their implicit bias was clear in the number of tenured or tenure track women the men hired (did I mention the number was zero?) The justification the de facto alpha male, call him B, of the department expounded frequently at faculty meetings for this gender disparity was the lack of women in the hiring pool who met the required criteria. In other words, the men in the hiring committee could find no qualified females to teach their desired type of finance. This sorry excuse for low female representation in organizations is now regarded as lame and inexcusable. B spoke for the group in most meetings and considered himself as someone who: (1) upheld meritocracy, (2) succeeded by his own merit, and (3) was in no way sexist. He was a big man, arrogant, cruelly dismissive, and possessed ostensible certitude in his convictions. B virulently opposed my teaching a course in financial ethics and made that clear at the start. Academic meetings can suck the life from your soul.

The room I entered was windowless, lit by two long fluorescent light strips, and contained a rectangular non-descript conference table around which sat nine men and one woman (she who initially recruited me, call her H). The non-tenured male faculty of the department did not think it politically wise to show up for this meeting—no need to jeopardize their tenure by supporting a female lecturer disliked by the tenured men. The atmosphere was thick with hostility when I entered the room. The men did not smile or greet me warmly if even at all. H looked down at her notebook. It was evident the men had already made up their minds and resented my impudence to even call a meeting. Anger rose in me against the injustice of this decision. Gamely, I made my presentation anyway, explaining all the reasons mentioned above and then waited for the inevitable rejection.

"We don't agree with you that our finance program needs a course in financial ethics. And the MBAs have a mandatory course in business ethics anyway." squeaked one associate professor, B's minion.

While B was tall, the minion was short, with sagging jowls and a pudgy figure. He leaned into the table channeling up his best Sheryl Sandberg, stared mockingly at me, and attempted an imposing and intimidating stance. He made a surreptitious sidelong glance at B to confirm he had B's approval. The posturing and sycophancy were sad, and I rolled my eyes mentally.

"We all teach ethics in our courses. We have said many times, we incorporate ethics in our lectures, whenever it's appropriate. There's no need to take up a precious slot for your proposed course" said B in an over-done stentorian voice, wanting to project power, intellect, and authority. This statement implied he knew moral philosophy well enough to teach ethics.

"We don't think a course on financial ethics such as yours will benefit the students. Ethics is infused into all our classes" interjected an older man, close to retirement, who fancied himself a sagely, senior, authoritative presence, proving humans tend to have the best impressions of themselves.

But his affected soothing tone was discordant with the hostility in the room. All the while, H remained silent, except for a deep sigh or two, throughout the meeting. There would be no support from my fellow female. The men made more patronizing remarks and demonstrated ostentatious indifference to my responses. A couple of younger males made placating and anodyne statements in an attempt to show a little decency. Finally, I left the room infuriated and humiliated. The next day I filed an official complaint to the university office that handled discrimination.

My Complaint

Most universities have a department that manages complaints on all sorts of discrimination and harassment. These departments operate under euphemistic monikers like "Office of Institutional Equity and Access," or "Office of Institutional Opportunity and Access." The acronyms are OEA or OIA, but many prefer the unofficial term, CYA. I filed a gender discrimination complaint with the university's, call it in plain language, anti-discrimination office.

Women are usually caught in a difficult place when they are discriminated against. We feel there is discrimination by men, but the mistreatment is done so subtly, we wonder if we have a case to file. Morley writes about her experience in the academy:

> I have also known colleagues who have applied their creativity to making my life as difficult as possible, in order to ensure that I never soared above them in the academic hierarchy. One former colleague, a total inactive in every other respect, always managed to manipulate structures, such as timetabling or representation on decision-making committees, to my disadvantage. He withheld important information, but made strenuous efforts to tell me anything that would unsettle or destabilise me. He infused every transaction with me with sarcastic, undermining remarks. Nothing he did was ever tangible enough to warrant a formal complaint – he always stopped just short of that point. To have raised these problems with my dean or head of department would have resulted in my being labelled oversensitive or small-minded. I soon learned from feminist colleagues elsewhere that relations such as these were widespread, and that there was nowhere to take the outrage and confusion that many of us were experiencing.[3]

Nevertheless, I filed my complaint with the assistant supervisor of the anti-discrimination office. A young man, he showed genuine sympathy and concern. I listed my grievances:

1. No tenured or tenure-track female faculty in the finance department.
2. A hostile male-dominated environment.
3. Implicit bias against women as seen in curriculum direction and choices.

An example of implicit bias is when male professors unconsciously view female lecturers, such as H, as handmaidens. Women would carry out administrative work and other service tasks, but with little authority in overall departmental strategy (such as it was).

The Dean of BSPU called me into her office soon after I filed my complaint. Clearly, she wanted this problem to disappear. She did not wish to upset the tenured faculty, whose backing she needed to stay in power. The clique of male finance faculty members knew I would receive no help from this quarter, despite the dean being a woman. The dean was chiefly a cheerleader for the school, and that role was just fine with the finance faculty. Thus, we observe two female archetypes lurking in the collective unconscious: the handmaiden and the cheerleader.[4] Carl Jung describes archetypes as consisting of mythological motifs or primordial images in the collective unconscious. The handmaiden provides support services to men, who have important work to do. The cheerleader applauds and sings praises to the world, of the achievements of men. The archetype for powerful intelligent women, who speak out, is the witch, or "monster" as a well know U.S. politician has called smart, formidable women who oppose him.[5]

My discrimination case went on for a few weeks, without any information given to me about the process. Ultimately the anti-discrimination office dismissed the case as they claimed they found no proof to support my complaints. The finance department was not even encouraged by the university administration to hire tenured females into its ranks. I discovered the outcome in an indifferent email I received from the supervisor (female) of the office. (I subsequently discovered the young man with whom I had initially filed my complaint was no longer working at the anti-discrimination office. I never knew if he had been fired or left voluntarily.) I resigned the next day.

ETHICS ISSUE: SYSTEMIC GENDER DISCRIMINATION, IMPLICIT BIAS

The ethics issue in this case study is systemic gender discrimination and implicit bias against women in the finance academy. My experience in this case is not exceptional by any means because systemic gender discrimination and implicit bias in the academic setting are well documented. Monroe et al., confirm the existence of a gender inequity problem in the academy.[6] Women earn less, are underrepresented in almost all disciplines, and men are more likely than women to hold tenure track positions, be promoted to tenure, and achieve full professorships. Another study, called the MIT Report, found young women begin their academic careers by believing gender discrimination will not happen to them.[7] Many initially feel well supported within their departments. They soon discover, however, working situations actually worsen with tenure. Tenured MIT women faculty described feeling marginalized and excluded from significant roles in their departments. Women faculty observed pervasive subtle institutional or cultural forms of discrimination, as well as individual isolated incidents of discrimination.

Increasing evidence shows much gender bias operates at the unconscious level. Even individuals who consciously reject gender norms tend to unconsciously evaluate women and men according to different criteria and to expect members of each gender to do better in those respects traditionally associated with their gender. This stereotyping is called implicit bias. In the MIT study, women described a legacy of male chauvinism, much of it sub-conscious or pre-conscious on the part of men, some of whom simply did not realize they were being patronizing or sexist. In the Monroe et al. study, one respondent stated:

> The most fundamental problem is the old boy network. These men have been here for 30 years and gotten into that power structure. They don't look for goals of equity. They have a whole interpersonal political structure set up to support their regressive values…It frustrates me that the administration doesn't want to address that.[8]

Looking back at the vitriolic resistance encountered when I proposed a new course, I now see the reaction was predictable. The curriculum is a crucial area where faculty exerts power over type, structure, and content of knowledge provided to students. Academics view the power over course offerings as a vital way to influence educational outcomes and the power imbues them with a feeling of stature. Thus, the curriculum illustrates the way in which hegemonic definitions of education, culture, and knowledge are contested. Feminists have decoded these secret complicities between power and knowledge identifying how power functions to determine what students had the opportunity to learn and what was forbidden to them.[9] At the BSPU finance department, a male-dominated faculty decided on what the curriculum would be, negating any input from women. In addition to financial ethics, I had suggested the following curriculum additions: micro-finance, environmental, social and governance (ESG) investing, and Islamic finance. The men summarily dismissed all these new course suggestions without any discussion.

Often, implicit bias puts women at a net disadvantage due to their gender. It is not very difficult to see the unfairness of implicit bias and of the ensuing differential treatment of women and men: implicit bias invites unjustified discrimination. Additionally, the imposition of different standards of evaluation of performance on women and men unjustifiably limits the scope of occupational choice, or at least of access, for some. The implicit bias of male faculty relegates women to providing service roles. The majority of female faculty complain about service, the label for administrative work in the academic setting. Women do far more than their share of service because this work is uniformly lower status, and not rewarded or appreciated by the system. The handmaiden archetype mentioned in the previous section plays perfectly into this reality. Across departments, women do a disproportionate share of service work.[10] Service is least rewarded and far less valued than research. Studies show that unconscious bias leads individuals to consistently and significantly undervalue female labor.[11] Why, then, are we to support the notion that academics would alone be immune from the same social forces that affect all other human beings?

The idea that the academy might be a violent place appears at first to be a bizarre juxtaposition, but Morley "unmasks" the myriad ways in which women are undermined and excluded from access to resources, influence, career opportunities, and academic authority.[12] We observed in this case how the university did not support my complaints on gender discrimination. The institutional climate in the academy is complacent about discrimination and harassment, preferring to keep things covered up by discouraging official reports of discrimination or harassment. Anachronistic practices and hierarchical structures form the basis of systemic gender discrimination and accounts, in part, for women's subordination in the finance academy specifically and the academy in general.

ETHICS ANALYSIS: FAIR TREATMENT AND RIGHTS

There are laws that prohibit discrimination in hiring and promotion. Equal Employment Opportunity (EEO) places responsibilities on employers of fifteen people or more and prohibits the stereotyping of jobs. In the finance academy, the implicit bias against women arises because society, in general, views women as being inferior at math to men. Sex stereotyping still persists in many schools, where girls are subtly led into some courses and boys into others. Similarly, the finance academy, like its economics brethren, subtly discourages female participation by its heavy domination of quantitative methods and statistics. Discrimination is often subtle. If for a position, powerful men choose criteria in terms of what skills white males are typically good at, they can write a job description that can be filled only by white males. Hence, we must ask, are the criteria themselves free of bias and prejudice? Are they fair? Discrimination built into job criteria is difficult to root out by law. But pressure can be brought to bear, by those within the organization, and professional associations, to rid job descriptions of built-in discrimination. Fair non-discriminatory hiring is not significant unless those hired have a chance to compete on an even playing field for advancement and raises. In these areas, the finance academy at BSPU had built-in prejudices and biases in favor of white males.

In Chapter 5, we discussed at length why gender discrimination is unethical. All ethics frameworks for the analyses of gender discrimination demonstrate the act is wrong and provide reasons why gender discrimination is unethical. Here's a recap of those arguments from Chapter 5.

Justice Theory. Justice is giving each person her due, treating equals equally, and unequals unequally. There is no reason to not treat women equally to men. From an ethics point of view, equal opportunity is a moral right of all people. This right is built into the two principles of justice developed by John Rawls. The one relevant to this case is the equality of opportunity principle: positions and offices should be open to all under conditions of fair equality of opportunity. This principle calls for equal access to all positions and offices. Gender discrimination is unjust because it violates the equality of opportunity principle. Another reason discrimination against women is unjust is the disadvantage imposed on the discriminatee, i.e., the woman. By disadvantage we mean whatever it is that ultimately disbenefits the woman. Common candidates for disadvantage are shortfalls in resources, welfare, and capabilities. Women become worse off relative to the recipients of the resources she otherwise should have gained (comparative disadvantage), and also worse off if discrimination had not occurred (absolute disadvantage).[13]

Duty-Based (Deontological) Ethics. According to Kant's framework of ethics, we must respect human beings as ends in themselves because every human being has dignity and is therefore, deserving of respect. Respect for people means fair and equal treatment irrespective of gender.

Human Rights Based on Religions. The oldest basis of human rights arises from religion. God confers inviolable rights to humans. These God-given rights, such as the right to freedom, and equal treatment are called natural rights. Women have a natural right to be respected, and to equal treatment.

Natural Law Theory. The prime moral directive in natural law is, in short, do good and avoid harm. In modern secular parlance, the fundamental principle of natural law becomes, "do good, avoid harm." Applying the primary natural law principle to this case, we find not hiring women and not giving them equal resources and opportunities does not (1) do good; nor does the action (2) avoid harm. To do good would be to help women succeed and achieve their potential by allowing them a place at the table.

Utilitarianism. In evaluating the amount of the good versus bad consequences of excluding women from resources, positions, and decision-making authority, reasonable minds will agree the bad outcomes outweigh the good ones (see Chapter 5 for a more detailed calculation). Women are harmed, as are men, when they are discriminated against because of their gender. Benefits accrued are few, asides from assuaging some male egos.

Sen's Capability Approach. Sen provides distinctive insights for ethical analyses of gender discrimination. His capability approach argues all human beings should have an equality of basic capability. This argument provides a moral justification for attending to and confronting discrimination against women in various aspects of life. What is important normatively for a woman's well-being is what she is able to do or to be, not just what possessions or income she holds.

RIGHT ACTION: SPEAK UP AND GARNER SUPPORT

In Monroe et al.'s study of gender discrimination in the academy, most respondents rejected overt and confrontational political responses to perceived discrimination. Instead the women favored a more adaptive discourse that both revealed a keen sense of the power dynamics in the university and prioritized incremental progress over cultural overhaul.[14] Few chose to engage in overt political responses that would actively challenge the structure of the Academy and university policy. Younger faculty, in particular, preferred to work "within the system" to solve gender inequality problems. This approach becomes understandable when set in the context of insidious institutional and cultural forms of discrimination operating through less visible dimensions of power relations. The discriminatory acts are not observable and in general, difficult to prove. Indeed, this chapter showcases the non-tangible forces aligning against a woman in the academy: systemic gender discrimination, unspoken power differentials, capitalist profit priorities, and implicit bias.

One suggestion for reducing gender discrimination in the academy is to hire women into positions of power and high status within the administration and departments. In other words, more deans, and faculty chairs should be women. However, just holding power is not always enough to ensure change. Often, a woman's holding of a high-level position would devalue or minimize the position, casting it into service mode, not power mode. This observation is made frequently across university departments so much so, it has its own label, gender devaluation. Gender devaluation refers to "the subtle process by which administrative positions lose their aura of status, power, and authority when held by women."[15] These positions devolve to be treated as service or support roles. For example, the dean of BSPU was a woman and yet, many saw her as mostly a cheerleader. Hers was a support role: to raise money for the school and make the faculty look good.

Therefore, ensuring the number of women in power positions reaches a critical mass, rather than just the one or two who become tokens in their work area, remains a vital goal. Women should strive to form groups or associations in which they can discuss shared problems of discrimination and harassment. These groups also help women find workable solutions to gender discrimination. Without support and advice from other females and female mentors, women in the academy will likely prefer to not complain because they recognize there are negative repercussions for those who push for change. Women feel it is a balancing act, to work for reform without making men feel threatened by change. Sometimes, women decide it simply isn't worth the effort.

Yet, those of us who can and are willing to make the effort of speaking out, should do so. I have few regrets about lodging an official complaint to the college anti-discrimination office. Since the #MeToo movement and the subsequent higher awareness and intolerance of gender discrimination and harassment, organizations are a little less likely to bury gender discrimination complaints. The outcome in my case was not what I had wanted. It takes time and consistent effort to wear down the boulders that block women's access to fair treatment. The Daoist thought, nothing in the world is as soft as water, nothing else can wear away the hard and the strong, applies to women's continuing movements against discrimination.[16] It seems reasonable to assume that as more women enter college departments in tenured professor positions, the decision-making dynamic will change. Just as water wears down rocks, increasing numbers of women in power positions erode inequality between the sexes, and society begins to shy away from its patriarchal structure.

NOTES

1. Transcript of Remarks at the 14th Annual John M. Ashbrook Memorial Dinner, Ashland University (September 11, 1997). https://ashbrook. org/events/kissinger-transcript/. Accessed September 29, 2020.
2. Nassim Nicholas Taleb, *Antifragile: Things that Gain from Disorder* (New York, New York: Random House, 2012).
3. Louise Morley, *Organising Feminism: The Micropolitics of the Academy* (London, UK: Palgrave Macmillan, 1999), 8.
4. Anthony Storr, *The Essential Jung* (Princeton, NJ: Princeton University Press, 1983). Carl Jung described the collective unconscious as consisting of mythological motifs or primordial images to which he gave the name "archetypes." Archetypes are not inborn ideas, but "typical forms of behaviour which, once they become conscious, naturally present themselves as ideas and images, like everything else that becomes a content of consciousness" (p. 16). Archetypes have an organizing influence on images and ideas. Archetypes are not themselves conscious but seem to be like underlying ground themes upon which conscious manifestations are sets of variations.

5. Juana Summers, "Trump Calls Harris a 'Monster,' Reviving A Pattern of Attacking Women of Color." *NPR* (October 9, 2020). https://www.npr.org/2020/10/09/921884531/trump-calls-harris-a-monster-reviving-a-pattern-of-attacking-women-of-color. Accessed October 15, 2020.

6. Kristen Monroe, Saba Ozyurt, Ted Wrigley, Amy Alexander. "Gender Equality in Academia: Bad News from the Trenches, and Some Possible Solutions." *Perspectives on Politics*, Vol. 6, Issue 2 (June 2008), (215–233) pp. 215–216.

7. MIT Report. "A Study on the Status on Women Faculty in Science at MIT." *MIT Faculty Newsletter*, Vol. XI, Issue 4 (1999).

8. Monroe et al. (2008), p. 218.

9. Morley (1999), p. 8.

10. Monroe et al. (2008), p. 220.

11. Rachel C. Sayers, "The Cost of Being Female: Critical Comment on Block." *Journal of Business Ethics*, Vol. 106 (2012), 519–524.

12. Morley (1999), pp. 3–4.

13. Carl Knight, "The Injustice of Discrimination." *South African Journal of Philosophy*, Vol. 32, Issue 1 (2013), 47–59, p. 49.

14. Kristen et al. (2008), p. 218.

15. Monroe et al. (2008), pp. 219–220.

16. Lao Tzu, *Tao Te Ching*, trans. Ursula K. Le Guin (Boston, MA: Shambala Publications, 1997), Chapter 1.

CHAPTER 10

Finance Academy Ideological Bias Case Study

The Story: Fear of Allowing Different Perspectives

The gender discrimination I experienced in the previous case study (Chapter 9) arose from systemic bias (prejudice built into the power, resource allocation, and institutional structure of the organizational system) and implicit bias (the subconscious gender stereotyping by male finance faculty). But there exists another reason for the cancellation and rejection of my financial ethics courses at BSPU: ideological bias. To have an ideological bias is to favor, consciously or unconsciously, a particular theory with its attendant assumptions and inherent set of values, holding firmly to the belief this theory embodies the true one among others. The prevailing ideology of the BSPU finance faculty draws sustenance and standing from the economic theory espoused by Milton Friedman in the 1950s. Free market capitalism counts as one name for Friedman's brand of economics. Neo-liberal economics is another. This ideology dominates the economic zeitgeist in much of the world. In turn, neo-liberalism has spawned three models of finance, collectively known as modern finance

---

Supplementary Information The online version contains supplementary material available at https://doi.org/10.1007/978-3-031-34401-5_10.

K. Tan Bhala, *Ethics in Finance*,
https://doi.org/10.1007/978-3-031-34401-5_10

theory or MFT: efficient market hypothesis (EMH), capital asset pricing model (CAPM), and the options pricing model (OPT).

I described and gave a quick analysis of MFT in the Bangkok Misadventure case study in Chapter 2. In that case study, I noted 80% of the students in my BSPU class thought it was not unethical to set up a client with a high-end prostitute. Two of the three reasons for their choice are connected to Friedman's theory. First, these students were taught and believed, as Friedman did, there is no need for moral evaluation in business transactions. Friedman's economics considers itself a positive science, a value neutral and objective discipline. In accordance with this view, economics and its stepchild, finance, deal solely with facts and draw empirically testable propositions from these facts. Economics and finance are independent of any particular ethical position or normative judgments. Instead, the market fully and effectively occupies the space of moral judgments. This intellectual position leads to the stand that finance professionals should not endeavor to offer normative, i.e., values-based opinions. Since the middle of the twentieth century, there has been a Friedmanite insistence in neo-liberal economics and finance on the primacy of profit maximization. In particular, the quantitative dimension of Friedman's theory is all the rage in business schools.

Second, my students reasoned the act was pretty much ethical; the equity salesperson can set up the escort for my client because the U.S. and Thailand are ostensibly free markets. Clearly, this argument is Friedmanite because it asserts the best economic environment for profit maximization is a free market. The high-end escort offers her services freely and the price she charges is driven by market forces. The client stands on the demand side of this equation and will accept the price if he is willing to pay. This transaction exists as one of millions in a free market and we do not need to intervene with ethical stop signs. Indeed, we are reducing a woman's freedom to obtain earnings from her work.

In sum, the BSPU finance faculty instilled free market, neo-liberal ideology in their students because this same ideology is fully embraced by faculty, who, in turn, were taught the same ideas by their professors, when they were undergraduates. In contrast, I propose the best way to come up with fresh ideas, that lead subsequently to new, improved policies is to have an ongoing conversation about different world views. Unfortunately, in this case, existing faculty who had a cherished ideology did not countenance other ideologies. New hires and courses needed to conform with the belief system of the department. Thus, if the faculty of the BSPU finance department were MFT disciples, there was no space for someone who teaches a financial ethics course because such a course is not part of the dominant ideology. The central ideological difference lay in how we wished to teach about capitalism. My course embraced stakeholder capitalism, the faculty espoused shareholder capitalism. If the academy, which supposedly nurtures new ways of thinking and inhabits the land of freedom of thought, behaves in a closed-minded, tribal way, we can therefore, not be surprised to find the same hardening of ideological positions in contemporary U.S. politics. Afterall, the 2020 presidential election results were violently contested by one faction, apparently urged on by the loser. This loser's fervent admirers continue to espouse one set of beliefs. The other half of the polity supports another set of values, and apparently there is no meeting of minds. And much like the BSPU finance academy with its predominant thought systems, no space for the other.

Ethics Issues: Exclusion Based on Ideology

Let's apply a utilitarian evaluation to the act of excluding a person, through hiring and promotion practices, because of her ideological perspective. To recap, utilitarianism requires the choice of an act that produces the greatest amount of happiness for the greatest number of people.

The positive outcomes of ideological exclusion in this case study are:

1. People within the excluding group who share the same ideology are bolstered by and feel secure in their belief the ideology is most likely correct and true because no one in their immediate environment and daily personal encounters challenge their ideology. The number of people in this group is not a small one because, in general, when one intellectual ideology is dominant, it usually dominates across most institutions of higher learning. Thus, if neo-liberal economics happen to be the prevailing thought scheme, then almost all economic and finance departments have faculty who are adherents to the ideology.

2. Investigations into the prevailing system of thought in a discipline increase both in depth and breadth as it becomes *de rigueur* to research, write, and publish according to the precepts of the ideology.

The negative outcomes of ideological exclusion are:

1. With no room for other systems of thought in a discipline, there is a lack of new ideas that may be better or hold greater veracity.
2. The dominant theory becomes ossified and then deified, making it even harder to change. Thinkers with other perspectives are further excluded from the departments because those who follow the dominant ideology develop greater certainty of the rightness of their thought system.
3. The dominant ideology continues to be applied in practice. Negative outcomes result from flaws in the theory, which then harm real people. In the case of neo-liberal economics and finance, the emphasis on self-interested behavior results in societal norms that condone the pursuit of self-interest in the belief such conduct benefits the market. Robert Putnam's provocative book, *Bowling Alone: The Collapse and Revival of American Community* chronicles the erosion of social capital in the U.S. The neo-liberal economic emphasis on self-interested behavior condones selfishness, not just in business but eventually in many spheres of human activity.
4. Not hiring people for holding different ideological views harms these people, who may become demotivated, not get high-level jobs in which they may have excelled or prevented them from doing innovative research that may have contributed to the common good.

In sum, the negative outcomes from the act of discriminating against people who have a different ideology from a group result in harm to people and society over the longer term.

To be fair, throughout history, humans have tended to hold tightly to their dominant systems of thought and have been loath to accept new ways of thinking. For a notorious example of this intellectual inertia, think of Galileo. This original genius was forced to publicly admit, under threat of ex-communication, his proposition the earth moves around the sun (heliocentric view) was wrong. Instead, he gallingly had to concur with the dominant geocentric view (every heavenly body moves around the earth). More recently, behavioral economists and behavioral finance researchers could not get jobs in economics or finance departments of universities. No high-ranked academic journals would publish their work. Daniel Kahneman, who won the Nobel Memorial Prize for

Economic Sciences in 2002 and is one of the originators of behavioral economics, actually worked in the psychology department, and not the economics department of Hebrew University. Kahneman's empirical findings challenged the assumption of human rationality prevailing in modern economic theory.

Ethics Analysis: Making Finance Theories Better

Since its inception in 2010, Seven Pillars Institute for Global Finance and Ethics, the financial ethics think tank which I founded and run, has tried to shift the dominant neo-liberal ideology emphasizing the primacy of profit maximization and shareholder value to a finance theory in which ethics plays a vital role. I have given innumerable speeches on this topic. Indeed, at the invitation of the BSPU careers office, I gave a lecture to students on ethics in finance, where I went through why ethics is disregarded by MFT. The content was probably so threatening to prevailing faculty dogma, I was never invited to give the lecture again. I have written articles and a book[1] to suggest this adherence to the ideology of profit maximization is flawed.

MFT should more accurately be viewed not as a theory but a set of models. If it were a theory, then it should meet the standards applied to scientific theories. Thus, if MFT is a scientific theory, it must have predictive value. And if this last proposition is true, investors would use these theories to predict stock price movements and score big on the stock markets, every time. Clearly, this guaranteed win does not happen. Even the best investors get it wrong because sometimes the stock prices of companies they buy for their portfolios do tumble. In other words, if MFT is a scientific theory, it does not meet the predictive criterion that determines the scientific-ness of a theory.

Second, the theories should also be verifiable, and according to Karl Popper, falsifiable. Once falsified, the existing theory should be modified or, if modification is impossible completely scrapped. Astonishingly, although the three "theories" that comprise MFT have already been falsified, they are still taught to undergraduates. The Efficient Market Hypothesis or EMH states stock prices already reflect all available information. This means the market has information on the economy, the industry, and the firm. Stock prices move as a result of this knowledge. Markets are efficient because they have already absorbed all available information and prices have adjusted quickly and accordingly. Yet, the idea that markets are highly efficient no longer holds sway in numerous quarters of finance. It never persuaded a swathe of practitioners in the first place. Warren Buffet being one of the more distinguished skeptics. Then there is the problem with the assumption EMH makes about how stock prices move. The model expects stock prices to appreciate through time at an average rate of μ per year. This appreciation is called the stock price drift. This gentle drift occurs because EMH assumes information arrives uniformly, in small steady increments. The new information causes stock prices to either fall or rise depending if the news is good or bad. However, this assumption, along with all the other assumptions MFT makes, does not accord with reality. Sometimes the news is so big and important the stock price surges or plunges. In a market panic, selling pressure is intense and positive feedback loops start operating, so a fall in price leads to a bigger fall in price, and so on. Instead of rationality driving the price, fear decides price movements. These types of events are not as rare as we think, and do not fit into the EMH idea of a smooth random walk. So, bam!, empirical evidence disproves EMH. This happens time and time again. Even if EMH were a scientific theory (which, no), it would probably have been discarded or improved 20 years ago. Yet, EMH continues to be blithely taught in the finance academy.

CAPM does not fare much better in standing up to the falsifiability test. A key element of CAPM is the concept of beta. The beta of each stock describes its tendency to follow market price movements. The greater the beta of a stock, the more it responds to a market move. According to CAPM, the risk of any investment is measured against the beta of the market to determine if the returns should be higher or lower. If we plot the expected return of an individual stock versus the return of the market over a number of periods, we get a straight line. CAPM derives an equation representing the line as:

Expected return of the individual stock =the expected risk − free return

+ the beta of the stock multiplied
by the market return
+ a random error term.

We can test the validity of this equation easily by using any stock to demonstrate if this equation works out in reality. Yet, in numerous examples, the two sides of the equation do not match up. Indeed, research on the reliability of the risk and return relationship put forward by

CAPM shows mixed results.[2] In other words, some studies have falsified the theory while others have upheld it. If CAPM is a scientific theory however, this ambiguity is enough to throw the theory out because in the end, we are left with no consistent, incontrovertible evidence the risk and return relationship dictated by CAPM is enduringly true. The best we may be able to say of CAPM is, the model can be useful in suggesting portfolios, *in general*, be diversified to eliminate unsystematic risk, i.e., the risk associated with a particular stock. By buying a diversified portfolio of stocks, the specific risks of the stocks cancel each other out. Therefore, in a diversified portfolio, a stock is theoretically affected only by market risk. Even this general proposition has its critics because there are portfolio managers like Warren Buffet, who think a concentrated portfolio, not a diversified one, leads to better performance.

If these finance "theories" are flawed, should we not be looking for newer, better models or at least improving the models we seem devoted to now, to help finance improve, so it can better the lives of people? I propose one way to incorporate ethics into finance is to start with purpose.

Right Action: Allow Other Ideas, Improve Finance Theory

Purpose is the end toward which actions are directed. Purpose guides and gives meaning to actions. Aristotle asked about the purpose of everything from medicine (health) to generalship (victory). Every action and decision is done for the sake of a purpose. The ancient Greeks, the Stoics, and the Christian Scholastics knew and lived by this idea and even in a postmodern period, contemporary humans still seek purpose, perhaps even more so than our predecessors. Just as many seek purpose to life, professionals in the broad sense, seek purpose in their work. A profession's purpose is: (1) a goal, (2) a reason for the work we do, and (3) a guide to decision and action.

A noble purpose is probably more likely to engender good acts, although it does not guarantee every act will be good. Some professions have well-articulated purposes. For example, the medical profession's purpose is to help people be healthy. The legal profession's purpose is to help people obtain justice. The teaching profession's purpose is to help people learn. It is therefore, not in the least odd for the finance profession to embrace a purpose. I suggest this purpose for the financial services profession:

The purpose of finance is to help people save, manage, and raise money.

Finance needs to have its purpose enunciated and accepted. Students in finance should learn it in their business education. Perhaps the purpose should be taught even earlier at the elementary level. Practitioners should be comfortable with the purpose of finance, knowing this objective implicitly and speaking it unabashedly. This acceptance and acknowledgment constitute a first step toward improving the theory of finance and thus, the culture of finance.

The improvement comes about through the crucial part of the ethically charged statement of purpose: "To help people." This phrase instills the notion of the "other" in finance. The idea of the other is where altruism and ethics begin. Secular moral philosophy from theories of justice to utilitarianism, concerns the other. The idea of helping the others also is widespread in religions from the Judeo-Christian, and the Islamic, to the Eastern traditions. Serving others is a basis of religious ethics. Christians are asked to love their neighbors, Muslims to show mercy to the less fortunate, and Buddhists to have compassion for all sentient beings.

Where finance has fallen over the past half century is its gradual abandonment of an acknowledged purpose that entails the notion of helping people. We have quantified finance for efficiency, and forced the discipline into a positivistic mode to escape the perceived quagmire of relativism. Quantification has led to the collective unconscious equating finance almost exclusively with money, neglecting the connecting link, people. So much so, spiritual leaders such as Pope Benedict, Pope Francis, and the Dalai Lama, feel the need to remind those who are inclined to listen: money is meant to serve people; people are not meant to serve money.

Articulating the purpose of finance clarifies, for everyone, the role and work of finance professionals.

Instead of having this erroneous connection in our minds:
Finance ⟷ Money
Which leads to this mistaken belief:
Finance⟷ Money → As Much as Possible for Me
We should have this clear and ethical connection:
Finance→ Help People with Their Money[3]

The statement and acceptance of a purpose is not the silver bullet that ends all unethical acts in finance. There is no silver bullet. Ethical progress is incremental more resembling an asymptomatic curve. But adding the concept of a purpose to current finance theories improves these theories.

To this end, it is heartening to observe the Business Roundtable (BR), an elite association of CEOs of major U.S. corporations, come up with a new statement of corporate purpose. The BR accepts that it no longer is the sole purpose of a corporation to maximize shareholder value. Since 1997, BR has endorsed principles of shareholder primacy: corporations exist principally to serve shareholders. To some astonishment, in August 2019, BR announced a new Statement of Purpose, which it says supersedes previous statements and outlines a modern standard for corporate responsibility.[4] BR believes the purpose of a corporation is not just to shareholders but to all their stakeholders. So, the new Statement of Purpose commits BR to the following:

1. Delivering value to customers.
2. Investing in employees through better compensation, benefits, and training.
3. Dealing fairly and ethically with suppliers.
4. Supporting the communities in which companies work. Respecting people in their communities and protecting the environment by embracing sustainable practices across businesses.
5. Generating long-term value for shareholders. Transparent and effective engagement with shareholders.

The common thread through BR's rediscovered purpose is the concept of serving the other. Among BR's members is one of the largest banks in the world, JP Morgan. Jamie Dimon, its long serving CEO says, "Major employers are investing in their workers and communities because they know it is the only way to be successful over the long term. These modernized principles reflect the business community's unwavering commitment to continue to push for an economy that serves all Americans."[5] The idea of service to others is therefore, now entering the consciousness of business, including financial services.

How else can we improve MFT to make it more comprehensive so it more reflects reality, and works off a foundation of moral principles? At this moment, there are three conceptual systems of finance: (1) Modern finance theory, (2) Behavioral finance theory, and (3) Islamic finance theory. Modern finance theory is dominant in much of the world. It is quantitative, systematic, and a useful way of looking at finance. Behavioral finance theory is getting well established but can do with more theory building. The theory explains empirical anomalies that counter predictions of MFT but still works from the latter's framework. However, behavioral theories account for human behavior MFT neglects. Islamic finance is inchoate, unsystematic, and lacks a fundamental quantitative basis. It depends on the formulas and models of MFT. Yet, its most imaginative, vital contribution is its unapologetic inclusion of moral principles to guide action.

Together the three theories of finance should be taught at business schools because each has a characteristic that a comprehensive theory of finance requires. MFT provides mathematical rigor. Behavioral finance accounts for human and group psychology. Islamic finance is guided by moral principles. A workable finance theory that unifies without syncretism, the three features of quantitative analysis, psychology, and ethics would be an enormous advance in financial theory.

Notes

1. Kara Tan Bhala, Warren Yeh and Raj Bhala, *International Investment Management: Theory, Ethics and Practice* (London, UK: Routledge, 2016).
2. Emanuel Derman. *Models. Behaving. Badly.: Why Confusing Illusion with Reality Can Lead to Disaster, on Wall Street and in Life* (New York, NY: Free Press, 2011).
3. Dr. Kara Tan Bhala, *The Purpose of Finance*. Seven Pillars Institute (January 22, 2013). https://sevenpillarsinstitute.org/mission/the-pur pose-of-finance/. Accessed November 16th, 2020.
4. Business Roundtable, "Business Roundtable Redefines the Purpose of a Corporation to Promote 'An Economy That Serves All Americans'" (August 19, 2019). https://www.businessroundtable.org/business-roundt able-redefines-the-purpose-of-a-corporation-to-promote-an-economy-that-serves-all-americans. Accessed on November 17, 2020.
5. Business Roundtable (2019).

Index

Ingram Content Group UK Ltd.
Milton Keynes UK
UKHW012209040723
424518UK00014B/340